FROM COP TO CONVICT TO CHRIST

*Lies, Deception, Corruption, the FBI Setup.
The Untold Story Revealed!*

STEPHEN LYNCH HARRISON SR.

Copyright © 2024 by Stephen Lynch Harrison Sr.

All rights reserved. No part of this book may be reproduced, stored, or transmitted by any means—whether auditory, graphic, mechanical, or electronic—without written permission of both publisher and author, except in the case of brief excerpts used in critical articles and reviews. Unauthorized reproduction of any part of this work is illegal and is punishable by law.

ISBN: 979-8-89031-914-2 (sc)
ISBN: 979-8-89031-915-9 (hc)
ISBN: 979-8-88640-004-5 (e)

Because of the dynamic nature of the Internet, any web addresses or links contained in this book may have changed since publication and may no longer be valid. The views expressed in this work are solely those of the author and do not necessarily reflect the views of the publisher, and the publisher hereby disclaims any responsibility for them.

THE EWINGS PUBLISHING

One Galleria Blvd., Suite 1900, Metairie, LA 70001
(504) 702-6708

Scripture Citations – In Alphabetical Order:

CEV
Contemporary English Version (CEV)
Copyright © 1995 by American Bible Society

HCSB
Holman Christian Standard Bible (HCSB)
Copyright © 1999, 2000, 2002, 2003, 2009 by Holman Bible Publishers, Nashville, Tennessee. All rights reserved.

KJV
King James Version (KJV)
Public Domain

MSG
The Message (MSG)
Copyright © 1993, 1994, 1995, 1996, 2000, 2001, 2002 by Eugene H. Peterson

NASB
New American Standard Bible (NASB)
Copyright © 1960, 1962, 1963, 1968, 1971, 1972, 1973, 1975, 1977, 1995 by The Lockman Foundation

NCV
New Century Version (NCV)
The Holy Bible, New Century Version®. Copyright © 2005 by Thomas Nelson, Inc.

NKJV
New King James Version (NKJV)
Scriptures are taken from the New King James Version®. Copyright © 1982 by Thomas Nelson. They are used by permission only. All rights reserved.

NIV
Holy Bible, New International Version®, (NIV)® Copyright ©1973, 1978, 1984, 2011 by Biblica, Inc.® Used by permission. All rights reserved worldwide.

NLT
New Living Translation (NLT)
Holy Bible, New Living Translation, copyright © 1996, 2004, 2015 by Tyndale House Foundation. They are used by permission of Tyndale House Publishers, Inc., Carol Stream, Illinois 60188. All rights reserved.

Thank you, Marvin Robert "Bud" Wohlhueter, MA, ThD, for your commitment and devotion in working with me on this book project. You took my life events and turned them into an incredible story, complete with devotional questions to ponder at the end of each chapter. Bud, you brought my specific events to light and turned them into spiritual truths and stepping stones for the reader to learn, grow, and develop into a mature follower of Jesus Christ.

Your voice and word selections as my guest writer were so profound and penetrating to the mind and heart. It was as if you stepped into my mind and chronicled my thoughts on how this book should come to life. God will continue to use you as you pen more books in the future. I am deeply grateful to God that He allowed our lives to cross paths for such a time as this. Now, **From Cop to Convict to Christ** can be read by the masses all over the world. Glory to God! Your friendship means the world to me.

To learn more about my friend, Marvin Robert Wohlhueter, visit his website: www.marvinrobert.com, or give him a call at 770.309.9200. May we both watch our lives change as a result of this manuscript. The best is yet to come!

DEDICATION

This book is a dream come true. After my years in prison, I truly believed that God would allow me to share my story. With that reality now, I want to thank those who helped me survive the jail days and those who are causing me to thrive today. Pastor John was instrumental in helping me keep my eyes on Jesus Christ during my incarceration. Additionally, Jack Owoc aided me financially for my prison term and had a job waiting for me upon my release in 2014. To my friends and family who believed in me and never gave up on me, I say, "Thank you." You gave me hope to go on each day.

To my church family, I want to say "Blessings to you" for allowing me to do life with you. It is remarkable for me to lock arms and live out the tenets of our faith in Jesus Christ. We are changing the world, one life at a time. For that, I am so honored to be a Servant of the Lord, God Almighty.

Lastly, I want to give God glory and praise for His one and only Son, Jesus Christ. His constancy in my life has been my anchor. Also, the Holy Spirit guides my steps daily. Where would I be without the Lord in my life! Knowing that God loves me and has a divine plan for my life brings great joy, comfort, and peace. It is this hope that I long to share with men around the world.

THE UNSCRIPTED LIFE

As we step into the dawn of 2024 with prayers and anticipation, considering the uncertainties of the previous year, let's embrace the comforting truth that God continues to hold the ultimate authority over our lives. This book is poised to extend a message of hope, God's Hope, reaching people worldwide. Although the details of our stories may differ, the constancy of Jesus Christ remains unchanged. As Hebrews 13:8 (NKJV) declares, "Jesus Christ is the same yesterday and today and forever." He patiently awaits an invitation into the midst of your life and circumstances, ready to transform your life journey.

Why is this transformation possible? The answer is simple. He is the Way Maker, Miracle Worker, Promise Keeper, and Light in the Darkness. The lyrics acknowledge, "My God, that is who you are." The song "Way Maker" gained prominence recently, resonating strongly as themes of confusion, hesitation, fear, anxiety, depression, and constant pressure characterize our times. Take a moment to watch the 2018 version of "Way Maker" by Alexandria's Pentecostal Church on YouTube—it's where the song first touched my life and undoubtedly changed it.

At its essence, "From Cop to Convict to Christ" celebrates the ultimate Way Maker, rewriting a story that was once held in death's grip, transforming it into a narrative infused with Heaven's promise. Hallelujah to the Lamb of God!

CONTENTS

Dedication vii
The Unscripted Life ix
Foreword xiii
Preface xv
Introduction xvii

Chapter 1	Hooray for Hollywood 1
Chapter 2	Mom and Dad 6
Chapter 3	Growing Up Catholic 11
Chapter 4	The Shadow of Shame 15
Chapter 5	Are You a Cow? 20
Chapter 6	Girls, Girls, Girls 24
Chapter 7	A Dream Comes True 30
Chapter 8	Meeting Dianne 34
Chapter 9	Making Ends Meet 38
Chapter 10	The Sheriff's Deputy 43
Chapter 11	My Dream Life Continues 49
Chapter 12	Just the Facts, Ma'am 53
Chapter 13	In Walks Kevin 58
Chapter 14	Little by Little 63
Chapter 15	Going from Bad to Worse 66

Chapter 16	Busted	74
Chapter 17	Forty Years to Life	92
Chapter 18	My Trial of the Century	101
Chapter 19	Going to Prison	115
Chapter 20	My New Life Behind Bars	121
Chapter 21	Soldier for the Cross	134
Chapter 22	The New Me	139
Chapter 23	Back in the <u>REAL</u> World	149
Chapter 24	Pointing Men to Jesus	156
Chapter 25	Was It Worth It All?	163
Chapter 26	Meeting Jesus Christ	168

About the Author 171

FOREWORD

Marvin Robert "Bud" Wohlhueter, MA, ThD
Author, Speaker, Coach, Counselor, Bible Teacher

I first met Stephen in the fall of 2018 as Free Chapel - Cumming had its informational meetings prior to the launch in February 2019. Needless to say, he had a commanding presence. Buffed to the max, his rippled body was hard to go unnoticed. Clearly, he was dedicated to his craft as a bodybuilder. However, the more stellar awareness was his compelling personality and desire to get involved and to serve the Lord in the local church.

Over the next four-plus years, Stephen and I have become devoted friends. We have spent many hours in person, on Zoom, and on the phone sharpening each other's lives with spiritual insights. I spent a year in 2021 teaching his Men's Bible Study with the tenets of my first book, *My Life Is: Real vs. Ideal*. Changing lives found us serving together many times over these past few years. I learned that Stephen had a divine story to tell and his book should come to life. *As the guest writer for his book,* Stephen and I are capturing his story and bringing it into print. I am excited for Stephen and the ways God will use his book to build His Kingdom. Glory to God as this book finally hits the world and the online pathways. *The best is still to come for Stephen!*

As you take time to read his story, just know that God can change your world too. He specializes in lives that go off course. In the midst of your challenges and pain, God welcomes the opportunity to join your storyline and bring a masterpiece conclusion. What have you got to lose? Ponder each chapter and dive into the words of life that offer spiritual water to your dry and thirsty soul.

Lastly, take time to answer the reflection questions at the end of each chapter. Internalize this book and learn about yourself while reading it. Don't rush past this part. An examined life creates a windfall of change. If you determine to "keep it real" with where you are and push into where God wants you to be, the road ahead will be one of blessing, purpose, and excitement. How is that for a few hours of reading this masterful book. Tell others about *From Cop to Convict to Christ*. Let's start a Revolution of Male Souls seeking their Heavenly Father. Enjoy the journey!

Sincerely,

Marvin Robert "Bud" Wohlhueter, MA, ThD
www.marvinrobert.com–visit my website!

PREFACE

Let's get this party started. Yes, I said party. It's a commemoration of epic proportions. That which lacked purpose now has a heavenly mandate. The mundane is now shrouded in the Divine. The untold story of Stephen Lynch Harrison Sr. is a fascinating and heroic narrative. The pages of my book will have you on the edge of your proverbial seat. It will leave you wanting to explore the following chapters. You will not be able to put it down as you lean into my story. *From Cop to Convict to Christ* is the progression of a life that started with great intentions but got blurred in the middle with *unchecked* living. No one ever sets out to walk this tightrope kind of lifestyle, certainly not me. Yet, all too often, one's ability to think rationally and rightly gets put on hold. Decisions become harder to shoulder as friendships get involved.

Even a seasoned police officer, as I was, is faced with daily ethical choices and integrity challenges in the thick of things. Right and wrong even get hazy as other officers are also participating in questionable decisions. Nevertheless, I always seemed to have a gut-level feeling that their behaviors were less than honorable and legal, for that matter. In the end, I was *lured* into a web of deception that was hard to escape. One unscrupulous event always led to a weightier, costlier incident. Like a man digging his own grave, I found myself in a whirlwind of deception, lies, unlawful activity, corruption, mafia-like men, and an FBI setup. You can't walk away from these mafia gentlemen at a whim. No, they don't play fair or care about you in the end. *The Godfather*, *Goodfellas*, and *Scarface* are not just movies to entertain patrons. They depict a real world that exists today, one filled with underhanded dealings and illegal activity. I was in its grasp.

How can one get off this deadly ride? The only way of escape is usually going to prison, but it could also be lethal if you are not careful. You heard that right! Neither one sounds inviting; however, at least prison keeps you alive. *From Cop to Convict to Christ* is not meant to be a catchy title. It became my reality. Arrested, convicted, and sentenced to 108 months in federal prison was my story. What? How was that possible, you may ask? Many do.

However, God had a more prominent storyline being written over my life, and going to prison was part of His master plan. No, God did not send me to prison. *My choices did.* Nonetheless, God does not waste any occurrence or situation to draw a person to Himself. That was undoubtedly true now for me. Yes, God gets the glory in the end as I, Stephen Lynch Harrison Sr., pursued the King of Kings and Lord of Lords, Jesus Christ, while behind bars. I may have met Jesus Christ as a teenager, but he became my life, heartbeat, purpose, and passion in prison. No more fair-weather Christianity for me. *I became a Soldier for the Cross of Christ.* There was no turning back, now. No retreats, either. My walk with the Lord was too personal. It had marked me. *My prison had a purpose.* Friend, so does yours, also for that matter!

Let us pull back the curtain and start at the beginning of my life. You can peer into the workings of my story and grow personally from my experience. Looking under the hood and kicking the tires of one's journey gives firsthand insight into what was working and, ultimately, not working as later discovered. You will never regret taking this excursion of action, surrender, and perseverance. You now hold in your hand, "dynamite." No, this one cannot destroy your life, as in the natural. Yet, my storyline is explosive, nevertheless. It is powerful in every way so let us turn some pages together.

As I said at the beginning, "Let's get this party started!"

INTRODUCTION

We all have a mental picture of how life is supposed to turn out. You know it goes something like this: college degree, marriage, two children (a boy and a girl), two-story house in a gated community, a family dog, and a white picket fence, to boot. Heck, why not dream BIG if you can have any script you want. That is just it. Not all hands are created equal. You see, everyone's voyage is unique and often unscripted. No dress rehearsals. What happens in life may not always be in your control or to a person's choosing. *What do you do then?* Do not rush past this question. *Have you been there?* Be honest. Are you there now? This trip, called "Life," has a way of getting your attention. It sure did for me!

I know you get it. I think that is why you picked up this book to read. I have not met you personally, but I would love to meet you someday. Maybe, one day I will. However, in some ways, I have met you. This title intrigues you. I can sense it. You are thinking, "Man, from cop to convict to Christ, how can that happen?" Does one go from good to bad and back to better than good or even great? Are there happy endings anymore in life's familiar story? Can I see a rainbow after years of raining on my parade? Do I get a second chance in my trek called life? Can my script be rewritten? Do do-overs become a reality? Your heart longs for a poetic ending just as I did. Keep on reading. It can! *However, it may take some time.*

How do I know with such confidence that it can happen to you, too? That is easy, in a single word, *God*. Please do not check out on me now. I am not going to get preachy or all religious on you. However, I must be honest and truthful. Yes, it was God who did it. The Scriptures make a bold promise in the Bible in Genesis 50:20 (NLT),

> "20 You intended to harm me, but God intended it all for good. He brought me to this position so I could save the lives of many people."

If you are not familiar with the declaration above, that is all good. No worries, here. It was spoken by a person named Joseph in the Bible. He, too, was in prison for thirteen years, yet he did not commit a crime. I know what you are thinking. But, no, he was innocent of the charge.

Nonetheless, he found himself locked up in a prison system. And, back then, it was not the four walls of today's prisoner who gets to enjoy working out, cable television, and earning college credits, but in a cave-like structure. It was by no means glamorous. Four thousand seven hundred and forty-five days to be exact. That is the equivalent of thirteen years. Day after day, Joseph wondered about his life. What went wrong? What led him to that point? Would it ever be different? All those are fair questions a prisoner would want to know. However, it's easy to gloss over our Heavenly Father's involvement in such dire straits. Joseph sure did, at least at first.

Guess what? So did I. Still, just as gracious, God began to meet me in ways that would eventually transform my life into a fully devoted follower of Jesus Christ, *a Soldier for the Cross*. I, too, could echo the words like Joseph of yesterday. What was viewed as bad would turn out for the saving of many lives! What lives, you may be asking? I'm glad you did. I launched a ministry called *Soldier for the Cross Ministries, Inc*. This men-based ministry was created to help men learn how to become a man, God's man, a Soldier for the Cross, if you will. I felt the need to give back to hurting men who longed to be whole in Christ, healed from past mistakes, and heading into a future of divine purpose and conviction. Why? Because that is precisely what I found in prison. *God met me. I met God.*

Let us start at the beginning of my life and chronicle the happenings of a storyline that is filled with intrigue, mystery, corruption, and scheming. Then, watch it turn the corner of dysfunction and embrace the wonder of God's healing, help, and hope in the world of Stephen Lynch Harrison Sr. Together, we will be forever changed as you read *From Cop to Convict to Christ*. Let us move on to Chapter 1.

1

HOORAY FOR HOLLYWOOD

"That's life! That's what people say
You're riding high in April
Shot down in May
But I know I'm going to change that tune
When I'm back on top, back on top in June"

Frank Sinatra, "That's Life"

My name is Stephen Lynch Harrison Sr. and I am saturated with American royalty. My middle name was from my father's side of the family, as Thomas Lynch was one of the Declaration of Independence signers. My last name is a link to two of our nation's presidents, Benjamin and William Henry Harrison.

Me?

I am just an American boy who was raised Catholic, became a good cop, and now runs a men's ministry proclaiming Jesus Christ to the world. *Soldier for the Cross Ministries, Inc.* is about helping men who need hope and encouragement for a brighter future. Through love and fellowship, men come to know Jesus Christ personally. We offer them tools and truths for practical living and being all that God created a man to be. It is inspiring and purposeful.

Oh, did I mention I also served seven years in a federal prison?

Yes. Honestly, I never saw that one coming.

I was born on June 14, 1960. Some exciting things happened over the years on my special day. In 1940, German tanks rolled into Paris and took control of the city. In 1942, a young girl named Anne Frank began her diary and my personal favorite; in 1954, President Eisenhower signed a bill to add the words *"under God"* to the United States Pledge of Allegiance. You go, Ike!

My birthplace was the name of one of the most famous locations in America. *Hollywood!* You have probably heard of it. We have many palm trees, the Hollywood Beach Boardwalk, the Arts Park at Young Circle, and the Anne Kolb Nature Center. Oh, wait! I was born in the <u>other</u> Hollywood, the city in Florida near Fort Lauderdale. There is no Walk of Fame or handprints outside a Chinese theater, and you will not see any movie stars hanging out in our grocery stores.

My book is not about celebrities. It is a true story of a guy, like you, who tried to do all the right things and wound up serving time in federal prison. *How is that for an introduction?* My life has been a rollercoaster, living the American Dream one day and experiencing an ongoing nightmare the next. It was being married to a beautiful woman with two wonderful sons and waking up to see all three of them gone like the wind. It crushed me. Nevertheless, *that is my story.*

Have you ever thought to yourself, "Dang, my life is pretty good. I've got everything I have ever dreamed of," and then...

Poof!

Like it never happened, gone, and you found yourself living every day with hardened criminals all around you. Yet, *that is my story.* If you like reading about surprises, heroes, villains, honesty, betrayal, patriotism, doing the right thing, tragedy, and unexpected twists and turns, then curl up on your couch and enjoy my life. *A lot of what happened to me could have been you.* Be careful what you ask for and who you trust. It could mean the difference between your rousing success and your abysmal failure.

Nonetheless, when you think your life is over, God steps in, breathes the Spiritual life of Jesus Christ into your soul, and puts you back on Heaven's path again. *Just like that!* Check out the verses that spoke to my heart while in prison. They are listed below:

> "But God, being rich in mercy, because of His great love with which He loved us, even when we were dead in our transgressions, made us alive together with Christ (by grace you have been saved), and raised us up with Him, and seated us with Him in the heavenly places in Christ Jesus, so that in the ages to come He might show the surpassing riches of His grace in kindness toward us in Christ Jesus" (Ephesians 2:4–7 NKJV).

As a Christian, do not miss the decisive significance for you here. The Word of God is promising the believer that no matter what happens on earth, for bad or worse, we are still and ALWAYS will be seated at the Right Hand of the Father with Jesus Christ, forever. *You can bank on it.*

In relatable terms, if your romantic relationship falls apart, you are *still* seated at the Right Hand of the Father! If you fail to win a major sporting event, you are *still* sitting at the Right Hand of the Father! In life, you might have to file for bankruptcy and be financially devastated. Nevertheless, you are seated at the Right Hand of the Father! If your spouse cheats on you, all your friends leave you, and your dog dies, you are *still* seated at the Right Hand of the Father! And, as hard as it may be to believe, if you have a bad hair day, you are *still* seated at the Right Hand of the Father!

Have I made this incredible promise from God Almighty to you clear enough here? Let that sink into your spirit. It has in mine. There have been many times in my life when I found myself at the bottom of the chasm looking up at nothing but darkness when my heart embraced that promise! It kept me going, knowing that God had the last word over my life, not my situation or present challenges. Even when it was wrong, or my days seemed blue with sadness, I knew that God had my back.

A Christian is not a perfect person. He commits his mind, soul, and spirit to God. The word *"Christian"* is aptly named. It means, "Christ in one." When people taunt me by stating, "Jesus is a crutch," I never hesitate to respond, "No, He's an iron lung. I don't lean on Christ. I depend on Him for *every* breath I take!"

Let us not be wishy-washy about this.

Jesus Christ is not my co-pilot. He is the only one in the cockpit. God does not share His glory with me or any other man. If you even suggest that He does, it is time for you to get back down on your knees and take a reality check. I am just happy to be alive and serving Him as His child. To God be the glory forever and ever! Amen.

"Bless the LORD, O my soul! O LORD my God, You are very great; You are clothed with splendor and majesty" (Psalm 104:1 NKJV).

I will always thank Him for my birth and the chance to live as a human being on this earth, a privilege that began on June 14, so many years ago.

~ Hooray for Hollywood! ~

KEEPING IT REAL!

1. The song called "That's Life" speaks of ups and downs. Does your life seem to fluctuate like that? Why? Or why not?

2. Royalty? Does your life need to be saturated in nobility to have meaning, value, and purpose? What validates you?

3. I served seven years in federal prison. God was using this to get my attention and turn towards Him. What is God using in your life to get your attention? Why?

4. How would you complete this statement: "I may have lost everything in a moment of time, but God _____ _____.

5. In Christ, you are seated in Heavenly places, no matter what. How does that impact the way you live?

~ *Verse to Memorize* ~

Start with GOD—the first step in learning is bowing down to GOD; only fools thumb their noses at such wisdom and learning.
-Proverbs 1:7 (MSG)

2

MOM AND DAD

"Dear Mom and Dad, I wish you knew I was trying."

My parents had a very romantic beginning. My father was in basic training at the naval base in Pensacola, Florida, and one night he stopped at a diner for something to eat. To his amazement, he beheld a waitress that took his breath away. She was the most beautiful woman he had ever seen. He smiled at her, and she smiled back. Frank and Adele Harrison were married two weeks later. In case you were wondering, they died still married over fifty years later. However, they were opposites.

My dad was a hard-bitten, tough guy raised in Bramwell, West Virginia's coal mining community. He was a no-nonsense taskmaster, only softened occasionally by his upbringing in a Christian home. He was an abusive alcoholic. My mother was as sweet as the pie she served at the dinner table, and unfortunately, she was too nice to the point of being co-dependent and dominated by my dad.

Of course, my two older brothers, Frank and Tommy, and I were also on the firing line of, *"Daddy not so Dearest."* When he got drunk, he pounded all of us. You did not please him or challenge him. You got out of his way. **Can you relate?**

"A man who drinks too much on occasion is still the same as he was sober. An alcoholic, a real alcoholic, is not the same man at all. You can't predict anything about him for sure except that he will be someone you never met before."
-Raymond Chandler, The Last Goodbye

It is an American tragedy when a parent is an alcoholic. The disease that systematically destroys the father or mother is even more devastating to their children. Alcoholism does not play favorites. It is a wicked storm that ravages the hearts, minds, and innocence of everyone living under one roof, and it impacts the entire family for the rest of their lives. Even after my father has been long past away, I have no idea what drove him to drink. There could be a myriad of reasons, but I would only be guessing.

All I know is that I have way too many memories of being beaten and watching my mother and brothers being assaulted as well. Of course, my dad was always contrite until he got drunk again, which was usually sooner than later. Like any good son, I always craved for his approval, but trying to win an addicted parent's support is as likely as a sea cow winning the respect of a school of piranha. Abusive alcoholics are a completely different breed from recreational ones. When you blend in that he had a dysfunctional father and was raised in a rugged coal mining town in West Virginia, then a nurturing father is a long-gone conclusion.

My brothers and I were on our own from an early age. I was close to my mom. I inherited toughness from my dad, but I got my caregiving, sweetness, generosity, unconditional love, and ability to give people hope from her. Unfortunately, I grew into a young adult without the wisdom and guidance of a father figure, and it proved to be costly in the terrible decisions I made and the people I trusted.

My mother, who had movie-star looks, aged far too rapidly due to the constant pressure and physical beatings she absorbed from my father. He even cheated on her a couple of times in their marriage, but being the kind-hearted enabler she was, she always took him back. She was a child's toy, a top spinning with softness, tenderness, and love. My dad was a top continually spinning out of control. As a result, I learned all about domestic terrorism far before the Oklahoma City bombing. I lived it on a personal level. I was the baby of the family. I had no support systems in place to cope with the constant rage all around me.

My dad was a bully. He not only acted like one, but he knew how to deal with one, too. One day, I raced into the house, quivering in fear, because a bully at school had chased me home to punch me out. When my dad asked me, "What's wrong with you?" I whimpered, "There's a boy out there who wants to beat me up!" My father glared at me and commanded, "Go back out there and beat the $#@&(*&&$()! out of him, or I will beat you myself!" So, I walked back outside and took the kid apart. I left him lying on our lawn bloodied and beaten. I walked back inside, and my dad said, "Good job!" That was my father!

> *"Childhood should be carefree, playing in the sun;
> not living a nightmare in the darkness of the soul."*
> -Dave Pelzer, A Child Called "It"

Sadly, because I was terrified of my father and his drunken rages, I never felt safe growing up. I wet the bed until I was twelve years old. *Fear is a powerful force on a kid.* Growing up, I was a conflicted mix of toughness and tenderness. My brothers and I played organized sports, and I grew into a champion bodybuilder. *Today, I can walk into a gym and impress people working out with my toned body.* But inside, I have always been a vulnerable, sweet boy who would not hurt a ladybug. I love people, and I would cross oceans to avoid damaging them. There are nice guys in the world, and I am one of them.

Later on, I became a professional policeman and a felon, serving time in prison; but, the real me was what I am today, a good guy who was always willing to give someone the shirt off his back. I always wondered what my life would have been like had I been nurtured by a gentle and supportive father. A man like that would have made all the difference in the events that occurred later in my life. I just learned to play the hand I was given every day. *How are you playing your hand?*

KEEPING IT REAL!

1. Your family should be the safest place on earth, but not always. What do you remember most about growing up in your family? Was it safe?

2. Were you "free" to be a child or thrust into survival mode? In what ways did you feel cheated?

3. A parent with an addiction changes the whole dynamic of the home. Did you experience such a tragedy? How did you cope?

4. Abuse in the home paralyzes a family's natural ability to love, embrace, and forgive each other. What are two things you could have done that would have helped to overcome your fears and help bring comfort and healing to your burdened soul?

~ *Verse to Memorize* ~

⁵ Trust in the LORD with all your heart and lean not on your own understanding; ⁶ in all your ways submit to him, and he will make your paths straight. -Proverbs 3:5–6 (NIV)

3

GROWING UP CATHOLIC

A father was reading Bible stories to his young son. He read, "The man named Lot was warned to take his wife and flee out of the city, but his wife looked back and was turned into a pillar of salt."

Then, his son asked, "What happened to the flea?"
I did not get that joke at first, either!

I was raised Roman Catholic. If you are a former member of the Church, you are already nodding your head. Love it or hate it! While growing up, Catholic life was never subtle for those of us who did. The first thought that comes to mind is the SWAT team of God's enforcers: *The Nuns*. Somewhere out there are the fragments of millions of broken rulers, now lying harmlessly in waste dumps, having served their purpose during those times of religious correction. I got my fair share! *My knuckles are still tingling.*

Then, there were the Cross's Stations (Stations of the Cross), also known as the Church's version of the Bataan Death March. The purpose of this religious ceremony, usually during Lent, was for all of us to honestly imagine what Jesus went through in his suffering and crucifixion. As a ten-year-old boy standing and kneeling, standing and kneeling and standing some more, and kneeling some more, I got it.

Yeah, Jesus suffered! What I always wondered about was, "Why did I have to go through all that if Jesus was the one who was sacrificing for me in the first place?" Doesn't my pain and agony seem a bit *anti-climactic* here?

Next, there was Confession. You go into an allegedly private box and stutter out your sins for the past week to a priest who supposedly has no idea who you are because you're shrouded in darkness, but once you open your mouth, your cover was blown. Now you are telling Father So and So, a friend of your dad's, all your shameful secrets for the past seven days, including the most embarrassing and humiliating violation of the Ten Commandments, **Adultery**. This revelation as a child to your beloved priest is a surefire way to make you feel like a scummy pervert. Why? The sin of adultery covers the entire gamut of sexual shame. Biblically, this is true even though you have never touched a girl or even looked at her. Remember, I was ten!

Nevertheless, if your buddy Tommy Reynolds got his hand on a Playboy magazine and flashed the centerfold at you for even a millisecond, you were an ADULTERER! If you accidentally saw one of your friend's moms walking down the hallway wrapped in a towel or had an impure thought after hearing a dirty joke, you were immediately categorized as the parish's deviant. Worse yet, you had to tell the priest all this without explicitly identifying the actual behavior or level of the offense! I was a kid, not Hugh Hefner. Geesh! I hated Confession.

Added to my boyish church experience, several of my buddies were altar boys. They would brag about sipping the wine after Mass and always informed me which girls in our class had weird tongues at Communion. One kid, I knew caught on fire during the service when he leaned too far over the prayer candles at the end of the communion rail! Several of the dads leaped over the railing and tackled him before the flames ate through his cassock.

If that were not enough, the Mass was in Latin. Like we knew what all those words meant! We did not attend Mass. We *endured* it.

Nevertheless, afterward, as we sprinted out into the parking lot, we always felt better about ourselves because we had been good Catholics. The Church was great at giving us treats after a good performance. Since I never went to Catholic school, I was required to learn all the rules and our religion at meetings called *"Catechism."* This learning allowed me to experience my first Communion and, later on, the sacrament of Confirmation.

Catholic living was intense, to say the least, even for a young kid. For my saint, at the latter event, I chose the name, Stephen. Someone asked me, "That is already your name. Why did you pick it again?" I shot back, "Because I like my name." What a stupid question, right? Catholic girls were always more chaste than the babes I knew in public school. You might get to second base with a Catholic girl, but it was unlikely. I believe they wore armor under their uniforms. My non-Catholic female classmates loved it when we rounded third and headed for home! If they had nuns for teachers, those rulers would be breaking every ten seconds. Trust me, just ask my knuckles.

Finally, even though saying the rosary was tedious for a youngster and I inhaled a ton of incense during Holy Week, I liked being a Catholic. It was a formal way of telling God you loved Him. Plus, all the statues of Mother Mary made her look "hot." She was like Miss America, in a robe. I always wished she could have been my mom. Nonetheless, since I thought she was gorgeous, I had to confess yet another sin of adultery to that darn priest. *Yes, growing up Catholic was not for the weary or faint at heart!*

KEEPING IT REAL!

1. As a young child, "Church" can seem confusing. How would you describe your religious upbringing?

2. Many say "Religion" is about instilling fear. Do you agree or disagree with that statement? Why or why not?

3. God has been described a Cosmic Killjoy, or a Holy Cop, sporting a big club to pound you. What is your view of God?

4. I enjoyed my religious roots. What two things did you enjoy about yours?

5. If God is for you, then who can be against you? How would you make this personal in your own life?

~ *Verse to Memorize* ~

³ Cry out for wisdom and beg for understanding. ⁴ Search for it like silver, and hunt for it like hidden treasure. ⁵ Then you will understand respect for the LORD, and you will find that you know God. -Proverbs 2:3–5 (NCV)

4

THE SHADOW OF SHAME

"Shame is a soul-eating emotion."

-C.G. Jung

As I grew older, I became more and more aware of a sensation that hung on me as perspiration clings to a body on a hot summer day. However, this feeling of mine had taken on several different forms; a little voice inside my head, a negative attitude, a sense of dread, or a belief that I was not worth much as a human being. This phenomenon would come and go depending on the following criteria: my circumstances, mood, an important event in my life, or a relationship that I cared about, romantic or otherwise. It could best be described as a *"Shadow of Shame"* that followed my life like a dark cloud, ready to rain on my parade of hope and success.

I could not shake its grip. It was ever-present, continually reminding me that I was a loser and did not deserve good things to happen to me. This shame I grappled with had an origin to it. It was not long before I identified how it became attached to me.

His name was Frank Harrison, and he was my abusive father.

Or, a more biblical way to say this would be "the spirit that controlled my abusive father was the mastermind." Yes, that is where my emotional and psychological self-hate found its seeds of life. All those years of humiliation as a child and a young adult were now part of my psyche, and I could not shake its hold on me. Like a virus or a tapeworm of destruction that enters your system, this humiliation was always there to remind you that you are never worthy of being loved, honored, treasured, or validated.

The Shadow of Shame.

Are you familiar with it? It is confirmed in every life, and it has incited many addictions such as alcohol, drugs, sex, gambling, and spending. This shame has been why so many people wind up homeless, penniless, mentally ill, or dead. If hope is the tonic for second chances, the Shadow of Shame is the dismantling of them. You may recognize shame's characteristics: depression, self-hate, low self-esteem, self-sabotage, borderline personality disorder, and a consistent path to constantly coming up short, no matter what your dream or potential. *The Shadow of Shame is personally devastating.*

It is like a barnacle on the bottom of a ship or a bloodthirsty leech preying on a vulnerable animal or human. This shame moves in following abuse of some kind. It could be a rape, incest, emotional, physical, or sexual abuse by a parent or partner, a traumatic relationship, living life or poverty in a third-world country with no hope, a searing event, or the culmination of years being told, "You are worth nothing." The past for many of us has been more than a little cruel. *Long after the victimizer is gone, the Shadow of Shame remains deeply embedded in our subconscious, ready to pounce whenever we come to any hopeful crossroad in life.*

If you have a new job interview that excites you, the voice of shame whispers to your soul, "You have no chance here. This position is over your head and beyond your talent." If you meet a potential love interest, you suddenly realize the feelings that discourage you, "Eventually, this person you love will abandon you, so you better make a move first because you are not worthy of being loved." If you finally find happiness in life, the Shadow of Shame will pound you daily with, "You are not there yet; you don't make enough money, your spouse can see right through you and will eventually leave. It may continue with, "You are a terrible role model for your children, and this is all going to crash and burn because you will be found out to be the fraud you are!"

The Shadow of Shame stops us from being successful at work, sabotages our relationships, and erodes our self-worth. *Worse yet, it is a big, fat LIE!* The bad things that happened to you in the past were usually the machinations of someone else who projected that sickness on you. He or she did this to survive the dysfunctional existence that haunts him or her. *Remember, sick people hurt other people.* Yet, now, you are still paying for it. Your mind is a battlefield, and your soul is bruised.

As I emerged from childhood to my teenage years, to young adult, and even today, I have been aware of the *Shadow of Shame* that began with Adam's sin in the Garden of Eden and wound its way, through time, into my dad, who infected me for life with it. This shame is not going away on its own. It does not miraculously evaporate. You must confront it and fight it until you kill it aggressively. You may do it through therapy, hypnotism, a twelve-step program, strong self-will, or a particular religion. *I did it through the cleansing blood of Jesus Christ on the cross that obliterated my sin and shame and the ensuing power of the Holy Spirit of God, who daily counters its ability to come back and try to get a renewed foothold into my soul.*

Nonetheless, growing up, I did not know Jesus personally, not really. As a result, I was at the mercy of being influenced by the wrong people, the power of materialism, acceptance from others, foolish decisions, and minimal purpose in my life. My father admitted to me once, "Stephen, I know I have let you down. I was not the father you needed or deserved. Of my three boys, you were the one who had the most love, the most to give, and the most potential for good. I did not encourage that. I am sorry, son." **Wow, that was years in the making but long overdue.**

It was nice to hear, but the damage had been done.

I would have to battle the Shadow of Shame with more powerful forces and people that had the power to overcome the emotional shell I had become as a man.

Keeping It Real!

1. Shame is a soul-eating emotion. Would you agree with that statement? Why or why not?

2. The Shadow of Shame: What comes to your mind with this title?

3. My origin was from my abusive father. What has caused you shame in your life?

4. Shame will not leave you without God's help. How do you control your thought life? Memorize this verse, "For as he thinks in his heart, so *is* he" (Proverbs 23:7a NKJV).

5. **Thinking new!** "⁸ And now, dear brothers and sisters, one final thing. Fix your thoughts on what is true, and honorable, and right, and pure, and lovely, and admirable. *Think about things that are excellent and worthy of praise*" (Philippians 4:8 NLT).

~ Verse to Memorize ~

Do not be wise in your own eyes;
fear the LORD and shun evil. -Proverbs 3:7 (NIV)

5

ARE YOU A COW?

Some say that your high school experiences are *"The Best Years of Your Life!"* They were not my best years, brother. I stumbled, bumbled, and fumbled my way through the first three years like a three-legged rhino at a prom dance. I did enjoy sports, sure. However, that was it. I was not a good student and the idea of having to go home every day to Mr. Volatile remains in my memory to this day. *It was horrible!*

If you have never grown up in an abusive home or with a raging alcoholic parent, you have no idea what I am stating. In that case, I am happy for you. You were blessed to have a serene, nurturing existence with parents who praised you and were consistently supportive. As I struggled in school, academically and behaviorally, I knew I needed a change of venue. At the beginning of my senior year, my dad finally did something sensible. *He enrolled me in a Christian school.* I guess he figured it could not be worse than public education and that we all had nothing to lose here. He was tired of me getting into fights and coming home with report cards that resembled Academia's version of *"Dumb and Dumber"*! Great movie, by the way.

My latest suspension from public school was five days, translating into a significant whipping, in daddy terms. I was sore for a week. My brothers and I were in a living hell. One night, my dad took the three of us to the garage and challenged us to fight him, one by one.

He began with my oldest brother. Frank backed down. Then, Tommy said, "Let's do this!" and got clobbered. I said, "No," of course. I was the youngest, but I was not stupid. Frank and I walked back inside the house with the maniac while Tommy lay there nursing his wounds. Such was the life of living with a drunk. *It was time for a change.*

We moved to Davie, Florida. I transferred to Broward Christian School at the age of seventeen because my uncle was the principal. It was soon apparent to the adult leaders that I was a troubled kid. *One of them noticed I was hurting on the inside.* Her name was Patricia Nichols. She was the wife of the pastor of the church that ran the school. The Holy Spirit told her, "Talk to that young man. He needs Jesus Christ." So, after chapel one day, I found myself sitting on a bench next to a woman of God who He sent to introduce me to eternal life. She asked me, "Stephen, do you know Jesus Christ, personally?" In my mind, I knew some things about the Catholic Church, but Jesus? Honestly, beyond the baby in the manger and the crucifixion, I was entirely lost here.

"Well, I was raised Catholic, Mrs. Nichols."

She smiled, "I'm not talking about the church. Just attending is not enough." I was puzzled. "Why not?" I asked. *"If you go into a barn, does that make you a COW?"* Now, I laughed, "I hope not!" So, for the next several minutes, she shared the gospel of Jesus Christ with me, finally asking, "Would you like to be sure you are going to heaven, Stephen?" I was all for that! "Yes, I would like to be sure, ma'am." She led me in prayer, and I asked Jesus Christ into my heart. It would take years to fully realize what that decision meant and how it would eventually change my life.

Nevertheless, I felt a little better for that day and returned to my dysfunctional life with Jesus Christ looking curiously at me. One thing was apparent to me, though: I *knew* I was going to heaven, and I was so RELIEVED! Thank you, Patricia Nichols. You were an obedient servant of Almighty God!

> "Do not let your heart be troubled; believe in God, also believe in Me. In My Father's house are many dwelling places; if it were not so, I would have told you; for I go to prepare a place for you. If I go and prepare a place for you, I will come again and receive you to Myself, that where I am, there you may also be. And you know the way where I am going" (John 14:1–4 NASB).

And, if there is any doubt here, you go!

> "But like many, as received Him, to them He gave the right to become children of God, *even* to those who believe in His name" (John 1:12 NASB).

I had a pretty good senior year. I joined the chorus to meet girls. Our group won state championships, but I just wanted a date. At home, things were still an adventure in Crazy Land. I would periodically get thrown out of the house for not respecting my dad's rules. I would sleep in my car, and my mom would bring me home and feed me, and I would sleep all day and leave before my dad came home—nothing new there. My brother, Tommy, now added alcohol and drugs to his repertoire. On Christmas Eve, he smashed into my mom and injured her shoulder. I defended her, and he stabbed the back of my leg as we went crashing through the screen door. My stab wound just missed a vital artery, or I could have died. *Merry Christmas, everyone! Don't all families live this way?*

Keeping It Real!

1. Making changes is never easy! How do you make changes? Be specific.

2. Changing environments is a key to growth. What environments do you need to change?

3. I met Mrs. Nichols in my new school. Do you think God had that all planned?

4. I heard the Good News of Jesus and invited Him into my heart. Would you like to know Jesus, too?

5. Jesus Christ changes a life completely! Check out this promise from God's Word, "[17] This means that anyone who belongs to Christ has become a new person. The old life is gone; a new life has begun!" *This offer still stands if you invite Jesus in.*

~ Verse to Memorize ~

The wise inherit honor, but fools get only shame.
-Proverbs 3:35 (NIV)

6

GIRLS, GIRLS, GIRLS

At age twenty-five, I finally found my dream job. In 1985, I worked as a bartender on the Fort Lauderdale beach during the famous Spring Break days. Are you kidding me? For a young guy who loved girls, I had the magic ticket. There were not only babes, but most of them were barely wearing clothes! Oh, my goodness!

You got to love Florida.

Every night, these beautiful girls came to my bar and smiled at me. They came in all shapes, sizes, and colors. It was like falling into a giant vat of M&M's. I would pour their drinks, make them laugh, flash my smile, and have my pick of any girl I wanted to be with for the rest of the night. I did not need a Playboy Mansion. I had a happening singles bar. I sure took advantage of the opportunities in front of me. Yes, indulgence was my middle name at the time. "Boys will be boys," as they say, and I did not waste any time living this dream life. It is what guys do, and I was no different. Sadly, that is what I was taught about manhood. Sex was a golden cookie to be enjoyed, right? Yet, things were starting to change me inwardly.

After a few years of fleshly obsessing and thinking this was the most extraordinary life in the world, a funny thing happened. *I became bored with it.* What was wrong with me? I was doing some soul-searching in my life. The *reality* was that I wanted more out of life than just pleasure. What? I can sense you thinking, "Stephen, what is wrong with you? You are killing it." Nevertheless, the hedonistic pursuit is an illusion. It seems like the world's most fantastic lifestyle, but it is not equipped to satisfy the human spirit.

It is just sex.

I was too intelligent, passionate, and committed to serving others to be fulfilled with temporary sensations, no matter how good-looking the women were. I wanted more out of "me" and out of my life. I needed to find a vocation that made me feel significant in life and society. There were many hurting people out there, and they required *heroes* willing to do the challenging work to make their lives safe and give them hope.

My father always wanted me to be a police officer. Indeed, this would allow yours truly to protect and serve my fellow man and offer myself for the bettering of other lives. *It resonated within my heart.* From that point forward, that was on my radar. I would give my best to a twenty-year career in law enforcement and retire with a generous pension, drawing 80 percent of my income for the rest of my life. That sounded exciting, fulfilling, and purposeful. My passion for law enforcement began to grow, and I learned everything I could get my hands on about being a cop. Life was meant to have an aim. *I just hit mine!*

Friends, let me take a few minutes to be honest, transparent, and vulnerable with you. I realize I might be taking a risk here, but I feel compelled to share this. Life was not meant to be about you, your carnal desires, selfish pleasures, and fleshly lusts. Sexual indulgence might satisfy your inner man for a while, but you will get bored with it, just as I did. No, God has a more prominent storyline being written over your life, and until you embrace this truth, you will keep pursuing girls, girls, girls, in vain.

Sexual conquests do not make a man out of you! *Hear me on this.* It is a lie from the devil and this world, for that matter. You give away a piece of your soul with each sexual encounter until nothing is left except an unfilled shell of a person. In your emptiness, you long for something more. Your life was meant to have meaning, value, and purpose. It is what I call the MVP life. Why is this so elusive? That is a great question. I have asked this many times. Here is what I discovered, as noted in Revelation 4:11 (NKJV),

> "You are worthy, O Lord, to receive glory and honor and power; *For You created all things, And by Your will, they exist and were created."*

Do not miss this declaration here. You were created and now exist for God's purpose. Every waking moment of your life is a gift from God about His purpose over your life. Embracing this truth brings liberty, freedom, and abundance. Lean into its charter. It will change your life as well as its perspective. Besides, your life also brings God pleasure as restated again in Revelation 4:11 in the King James Version (KJV),

> "Thou art worthy, O Lord, to receive glory and honor and power: for thou hast created all things, **and for thy pleasure, they are and were created.**"

Dear reader, you may wonder if your life matters to anyone, much less God, but the above verse settles the score. You are a pleasure to your Heavenly Father. No, every aspect of your current storyline may not bring out God's best for your life, but He still finds you delightful as His creation and is working to rewrite your story for His glory. Let us face this fact: We are wrapped up in Him. Without Him, we are a ship without a rudder, moving aimlessly through the waters of life. You exist for God. This verse is recorded in Acts 17:28 (NKJV) and seals the deal over our lives,

> "28 for in Him, we live and move and have our being, as also some of your own poets have said, 'For we are also His offspring.'"

WOW! Did you receive that into your spirit? You may have never read that before, or if you have, it has been a long time. Secondly, you may struggle with appropriating its truth. Nevertheless, it is your umbrella over your life. It is your covering. Think of each of the three pronouncements individually. They all start with the awareness of "In Him . . . "

First, "you live." Think about that for a minute. He is your source of life. He is your starting point. You exist because He wills it, so as the above Scriptures alluded. Secondly, "you move." In other words, the movement of your life functions as it relates to Him. It is not just enough to "live" or exist, but you must also "move" according to His rhythm for your life. Have you ever seen the word "GUIDANCE"? Many break this down to mean "G" – God, "U" – You, and "I" – myself, DANCE. In other words, it becomes a sharing of moves for His eternal purpose. Lastly, "you have your being." Do not miss this announcement. Your self-worth and self-esteem are wrapped up in Him, alone, and that is GREAT news. Many will shout otherwise about you. Nonetheless, your Heavenly Father states your value is found in being His creation.

Read the above verse again and again until it becomes a part of your DNA. Everything in life is sourced "in Him." Your living, movement, and being all converge into God's presence and purpose over your life. So, no matter what is presently happening in your world, the willingness to proclaim this over your life changes everything, moving forward. *Yes, He is the Creator of the Universe, but He knows you by name!* He knows the number of hairs on your head, and He has confirmed your days from end to beginning. That, my friend, is good news.

To further solidify this truth, look on YouTube for the song called "Every Sparrow." Bud used to play in a band called Kindred Heart. The singer, Sammy Price, wrote this song in the early '90s. In its lyrics, it speaks of God knowing your name. As *"Every Sparrow"* that falls, He knows them all. Yes, God knows your name personally. For thirty years, it was never recorded and released, until March 2023. To watch the song, go to Bud's website and click on the tab simply noted as called Sparrow: *See www.marvinrobert.com.*

Let us roll on to Chapter 7.

KEEPING IT REAL!

1. What have you been taught about manhood? Is it all about how many women you enjoy? Why or why not?

2. Could one really get "bored" with sex as I did? What do you think caused this?

3. Made for More—Do you believe God has an eternal story written over your life? Have you embraced it?

4. Here is a biblical manhood verse to memorize, "[11] When I was a child, I talked like a child, I thought like a child, I reasoned like a child. *When I became a man, I **stopped** those childish ways*" (1 Corinthians 13:13 NCV). What behaviors do you need to stop?

~ Verse to Memorize ~

[21] With persuasive words she led him astray; she seduced him with her smooth talk. [22] All at once he followed her like an ox going to the slaughter, like a deer stepping into a noose [23] till an arrow pierces his liver, like a bird darting into a snare, *little knowing it will cost him his life.* -Proverbs 7:21–23 (NIV)

7

A DREAM COMES TRUE

It was 1989, and time for me to grow up and become an adult. I decided to become a police officer. Luckily, my father had a drinking buddy, who also just happened to be the mayor of our city. He asked his friend, "I want you to help my son become a cop." The next thing I knew, I was applying to become a policeman for the city of Pembroke Pines, Florida. I was on my way to a new life until the interview. It all stopped with a straightforward question that tripped me up, "Have you ever taken anabolic steroids?" This question rocked my world in an instant.

I could have lied and gotten away with it, but I was raised to tell the truth, and so I admitted, "Yes, I had tried them." Just like that, I was disqualified. The interview was over. My plans were thwarted. My dreams were crushed. Now what?

Nevertheless, because the mayor was doing my father a favor, which got me the interview in the first place, I was told that I could *reapply* in six months with no further disclosure necessary. So, my plans to become a law enforcement officer didn't come to fruition, at least for now. I did not return to the nightclub gig. Why? I honestly thought that was a dead-end waiting to happen. Plus, God was trying to get my attention concerning my behavior and doing what honors Him. Yes, girls are great. Nonetheless, I wanted to live an honorable life, one pleasing to God, at least in some part. Thus, I continued to ponder my subsequent vocational pursuit. Help me, Lord! I feel stuck.

I was learning that LIFE does not work like a vending machine. You know how it works. First, you walk up and put in your money. Next, you select "Amazing Job" for $2. Lastly, you pull the handle. Then, out pops your request. **Wouldn't that be wonderful?** *If only life worked out that way!* Heck yeah, because then, you would next select "Great Marriage" for $5. Follow that with "Nice Home" for $20. To round things out, you would put in $25 for "Two Lovely Children." *Shazam*, you now have your "dream life" created with a few pulls of some handles. Vending machine living would take the world by storm. Even the makers of such machines would have captured the stock market with their remarkable product. Then, watch out for Apple, Google, Facebook, and Amazon!

You know I am being silly here, but you get my drift. I was learning that my script was not always to my outcome. I, like you, was led to believe that LIFE should play out just as I wished. Boy, was I wrong? Believe it or not, I never regretted telling the truth that day about my use of steroids. Honesty mattered to me, and I was not going down the rabbit trail of lies to acquire this law enforcement job. Yet, I needed to land on something to provide for myself. I knew God would deliver if I opened my eyes to what was around me. Also, I must be willing to offer myself its opportunity, even if it was not my ideal job at this moment.

Let us touch on the subject of "waiting" for a few minutes. How do you handle waiting about something you are pursuing or dreaming of doing? Be transparent and vulnerable here. No one likes to wait for anything in life. I get that. But waiting is a part of life and certainly a part of a bigger plan being written over your life. What is your waiting posture? Do you see waiting as inactive and casual? Or, do you see waiting as active and engaging? Is waiting even unnecessary? Do you find an alternative route in life when caused to stay for the moment?

Could God be using waiting to groom you for the blessing when it comes? These are all fair questions to ask.

From my own experience, God's plans are perfect, and His timing is impeccable. Do not rush the process seeking only to get the prize. For, it is the process that makes the reward all the sweeter if you are willing to wait on God's best. Counterfeit living will leave you frustrated and empty in the end. Satan always offers a "quick" route, but only God provides the satisfying and sanctifying one. There are no shortcuts to noble living. In the end, waiting gives clarity and confidence with a spirit of worship and surrender to God's divine plan over your life.

I truly believed I would become a police officer in God's timing, but I took a job working in the insurance business with a friend for now. My people skills and my internal drive as an entrepreneur made me successful at this job. I loved it because I enjoyed working with people and making a difference in their lives. Besides, I considered it a blessing to offer something that made individual lives feel more protected and safer. Not to mention, it would prepare me for what would happen next: *Meeting Dianne.* Chapter 8 awaits.

KEEPING IT REAL!

1. What causes you to dream? A job? A marriage? A new opportunity? A healthier body? A new car? A vacation home?

2. I was honest about my use of steroids. What would you have done?

3. The interview was over. The dream lost. What next? How do you process life's setbacks?

4. Waiting—What is your waiting posture? Is it necessary? Why? Could God use it for your good?

5. *God thinks differently than you do!* Memorize Isaiah 59:8–9 (NIV), "[8] For my thoughts are not your thoughts, neither are your ways my ways," declares the LORD. [9] "As the heavens are higher than the earth, so are my ways higher than your ways and my thoughts than your thoughts." *Did you catch that?*

~ Verse to Memorize ~

Let the wise listen and add to their learning, and let the discerning get guidance. -Proverbs 1:5 (NIV)

8

MEETING DIANNE

"The moment I saw her, a part of me walked out of my body and wrapped itself around her. And there it remains."

-Arundhati Roy

I was on a date one night in 1990 with a sweet girl named Betty Jean. We were not lovers, but just friends. We went to a bar and were having drinks when I looked over and saw a blonde angel.

Her name was Dianne.

Brown eyes, long blonde hair, and looked like the All-American Goddess. I was smitten. I could not stop staring at her. I also could not help noticing the gaggle of guys crowded around her, trying to get her attention. Boy, she was something. She had me, oh yeah! That moment was so etched in my memory. I even remembered the song that was playing while I fixed my eyes on her. It was "The Dance" by Garth Brooks. Betty Jean asked me, "Steve, are you *okay?*" No, I was not.

From the moment I first saw Dianne, the rest of the female population in the universe disappeared. In my mind, I began dating her immediately! Fortunately, Betty Jean knew the angel and did the introductions. It was not long before I was alone with this beauty and asking her out. "Can I have your phone number?" I queried. Dianne warmly smiled at me and said, "I never give a guy my phone number." I persisted, "Maybe, this one time?" She laughed, "You can call me at work." A man must learn to pick his battles. I was no dummy. She was worth it.

I called her at work, and we set up a date to go to a line dancing class the following Wednesday. I arrived there early and staked out a position behind a post so I could observe her. I wanted to see what kind of girl she was around other people. I wanted a lady, not a bar girl or a flirt. After thirty minutes, I was convinced, "She was the girl for me!"

Now, I had to ramp up the romance. I had a motivational aphrodisiac in mind for Dianne. I asked, "How would you like to go to Disney World?" She was all over that offer. "I would love to!" she purred. Thank God for Mickey Mouse. We planned to experience a two-day excursion, which included two nights at the Disney Resort. That way, if we were having fun at the park, we could continue the romantic momentum all night long. She agreed to that, too. I was, *"The Happiest Boyfriend on Earth!"*

Our two days with Mickey, Minnie, and the speed freaks that obsessively kept the park clean with their rapid-fire dustpans began a courtship that resulted in me getting her father's blessing for marriage. Eventually, I moved into her parents' house, and we lived in one of their bedrooms. Over the next three years, Dianne and I would remain single but lived like husband and wife. I will not lie to you. There were still times when I missed those nights meeting other women at bars, but like they say, *"The grass is not always greener on the other side,"* right? I remained faithful to my girl, Dianne.

Then, on one mysterious day, she visited me at work. I stood up and embraced her. Dianne took my hand and led me to a back office. Once there, she turned and looked up at me with her beautiful brown eyes and said, "I'm pregnant." After I picked myself off the floor, I mumbled to her, "We need to think this through. We have not been together that long. I mean, I'm not *ready* for all this." That was another way of saying,

"*Yeah, I was stupid.*"

There were so many preventive measures I could have taken and had not. Now, I had to face the consequences of my irresponsible actions. Intellectually, I knew I had to step up and do the right thing. Nevertheless, it took me a month to *emotionally* process all of it. *The free-wheeling Steve Harrison was gone forever.* It was time for me to be an adult. Pregnancy is a great motivator. I welcomed the challenge of being a husband and father. I wanted to give my son what a father should be.

Dianne and I got married on September 11, 1993. Our wedding was a hoot! We had an Elvis impersonator, and my buddies all came and got drunk. Dianne wore a more oversized wedding dress to hide her pregnancy, so our priest had no idea. Had he known she was expecting, we would not have been allowed to marry in the Catholic Church. To add a little fun at our "shotgun wedding," we took pictures of her dad dressed up as a moonshiner with a shotgun pointing at me during the reception. Thank God the priest was not there!

Dianne and I honeymooned in Cancun and had a great time. When we went to the airport for our return flight home, many natives shouted *"Rambo"* at me as I walked by. I guess it was my muscles. That was hilarious! Once home, we settled in and became a great family. I was in love with a simple girl whose goal in marriage was to stay at home, be a mom, and take care of her family. That had always been her dream, and now she was living it. I resumed my job as an insurance salesman and plotted my next job move. I was not climbing the ladder of success, but I wasn't mired in career quicksand, either. I was just your average guy trying to figure out things as I went along. *I was a typical American boy and a new dad. It was exciting.*

KEEPING IT REAL!

1. Meeting Dianne changed my life. What was a life-changing moment for you?

2. With my heart invested, I was committed to Dianne. Can you remember what that was like for you in a relationship?

3. "I am pregnant." Those are not exactly the words I was expecting to hear. Why was my stepping up necessary for Dianne?

4. Life has a way of providing growth moments. What have you experienced that changed your life? What did you do about it?

~ Verse to Memorize ~

Let love and faithfulness never leave you; bind them around your neck, write them on the tablet of your heart. [4] Then you will win favor and a good name in the sight of God and man.
-Proverbs 3:3–4 (NIV)

9

MAKING ENDS MEET

After the unsuccessful police interview, as noted earlier, I needed to land something quick. I began working for a friend of mine in the insurance business, as penned earlier. I enjoyed the opportunity, plus I was good at it. I took the state examination to become a licensed insurance agent in the state of Florida. My first assignment was working in an auto dealership as their insurance agent. Then, I followed a friend over to Allied Auto Insurance and made a great commission at $5,000 a month. This paycheck was good money for a twenty-something, and I worked my insurance gig until 1994. I was making a difference for others.

Life was good for many years, but then the bottom fell out. The company began to fiddle around with my commission structure, and my paycheck plummeted. I needed to find a more stable job to support the two most influential people in my life, my wife and my son. It motivated me to excel for my family's sake. My wife and I were building a home and a future together. My son needed a dad who would model responsibility, commitment, and protection. I wanted to be all of those for him. He deserved that kind of father, even though I grew up without it in mine.

A year after my marriage to Dianne, I left the insurance business. In 1994, I began to work for my dad, who owned his own pest control company. By this time, he had sobered up. We were rebuilding our relationship and mending fences, as it were. While not perfect, we were getting along great. I cherished this time of learning more about my father, and he was learning more about me. I would not trade that time with him.

Nonetheless, after two years of killing bugs, I decided to give the police force another try. As I looked back at that time in my life, I realized that I was not ready to be a police officer. We all know that young people do not grow up overnight. It takes time and experience, as well as overcoming challenges to build a foundation of wisdom and toughness in life, especially for a career in law enforcement.

By this time, I was mentally and emotionally ready for the road ahead in police work. I knew it would be challenging for me. It would also be difficult for Dianne to have a husband putting his life on the line daily to protect and serve his community. Going into law enforcement is a calling, much like a minister feels called to serve God and lead a congregation. In my spirit, I felt this was my purpose in life, and I wanted to give it my all. Now that I had my chance to prove myself, I would not let this one slip away. Finally, it was MY time.

Let us pause on my story and reflect on your narrative. As was mentioned, I dreamed of being a cop. This career caught my eye and filled my soul. However, notice I worked nearly five years in the insurance business and two additional years in the pest control industry. That is a total of seven years of my work life, almost an entire decade, given to something other than my prime interest. Wait, that is not how life is supposed to work. What was I missing? I wanted to know. *I suspect you do too!*

It would be easy to feel that I was wasting my time doing other jobs rather than living out my dream life. Can you relate to that? *Do you feel like you are misplaced somewhere?* The idea that work is wasting time is akin to a bodybuilder starting with lighter weights as he makes his way to more vigorous workouts. *Nothing is ever wasted.* God uses these times to build character, grit, dedication, strength, and clarity. Yes, it is not the desired outcome. However, the growth that comes from leaning into your job, no matter what it is, is priceless.

You can think of it this way to help you process. When you have a wife and child to care for and provide for, it is a selfless act to rise daily and give it your best at work. This act of responsibility creates muscle, a devotion muscle. The outcome of this level of obligation is maturity. Yes, "Manly Maturity" is needed as a husband and a father. What sets the young adult apart from the older adult? In a single word, it is *responsibility*. What if we broke down responsibility into two words: 1.) Respond, and 2.) Ability. You are growing in your **ability to respond** to any and every situation. As a mature husband and father, your enthusiasm and wisdom applied to all under your care give the successful effects that your family needs. Husbands matter. Dads matter, too! It is just that simple. Both wife and child need you to be stable and selfless.

What does that look like, practically? For starters, you do not get a pass when you do not feel like going to work. The sun may be shining, but you can go fishing on Saturday, not calling out on Wednesday. The sporting event that lasts into the morning's early hours gets passed up because you can not afford to drag into work the following day, feeling tired and less productive. Your best friend asks you to go on a hunting trip, and you want to call out sick for a few days to make it happen. What is the right thing to do? Go to work! That honors God and gives you favor with your employer. Yes, you are halfway to godly maturity just by showing up faithfully. It speaks volumes of your character!

You may be wondering, "Why would God allow you to work in something else if it is not your calling?" That is a fair question. Nonetheless, in the Bible, many are called to do something specific for God, and then it takes years of planning before the actual assignment begins. Take the Apostle Paul, who wrote most of the New Testament, for example. God called him to share Jesus Christ with the Gentile people. However, after his conversion to Christ, he spent seventeen years in homework mode. You read that correctly. Seventeen years of isolation and training would weary some of us out of the mission. One's interest may wane, and his or her investment into the vision may grow cold. Why? *We feel waiting is pointless to the process.*

Nevertheless, God permits waiting as a refining method that is invaluable to the spiritual result. It cannot be overlooked. *It would be best if you had it.* God uses this time to purge you!

After seven years of waiting, I was stepping into my dream calling. It was right on time in God's calendar for my life. At this time, the majestic would occur. At this moment, the outcome would be different. With this convergence of grace, the story would be for greater glory, God's glory. The heart of the matter was the matter of the heart. A different perspective comes during the waiting season. That is precisely the point in God's economy. Lean into your waiting. Do not curse it. Instead, embrace it. When you do, the favor of God becomes your launching pad.

Friend, make this chapter personal. Take some time and ask yourself, "Do I feel life is passing me by while I am waiting?" What is God trying to work into your life? What is God trying to weed out of your life in this process? Nothing is random. God has a laser focus when it comes to the things that can shipwreck your life. His hand of grace and mercy is to work on you and in you during the season of waiting. It may feel non-productive. However, it is doing more than you give it credit for creating. *Next, let us dig into my dream life in Chapter 10.*

KEEPING IT REAL!

1. Do you work with a sense of God's provision over your life? How?
2. I never lost sight of my dream job. Have you given up on yours? Why?
3. No one likes to wait these days! What is God teaching you while waiting?
4. The process of change takes time. Why do you think this is so?
5. *We feel waiting is pointless to the process.* "[18] Then, after three years, I went up to Jerusalem to get acquainted with Cephas and stayed with him fifteen days. [1] Then after fourteen years, I went up again to Jerusalem, this time with Barnabas. I took Titus along also" (Galatians 1:18, 2:1 NIV). Would you have invested for seventeen years as Paul did?

~ Verse to Memorize ~

When pride comes, then comes disgrace,
but with humility comes wisdom. -Proverbs 11:2 (NIV)

10

THE SHERIFF'S DEPUTY

I was honest. I was noble. I was rejected.

Now, I had another chance to fulfill my dream job. I was not going directly into police work, but slipping in the side door through the Department of Corrections. In 1996, I applied to become a sheriff's deputy, which entailed an introductory training course that involved physical and mental excellence. I had no problem with the first part, but I had never been a good student. It was time for me to become one or kiss my "dream" goodbye forever.

The course curriculum was daunting. The classes were set up in blocks with x number of hours defining each subject matter. An applicant was required to learn the following courses for starters,

    Communications
    Officer Safety
    Supervising in a Correctional Facility
    Responding to Incidents and Emergencies
    First Aid for Criminal Justice Officers
    Criminal Justice Firearms
    Criminal Justice Defensive Tactics
    Officer Wellness and Physical Abilities

Note the other 50 percent of the training was just as grueling!

What was even more challenging was my age. Most of the candidates were in their early twenties. I was the oldest applicant in the class at thirty-six years old. I had my work cut out for me. Nevertheless, I graduated with honors. I was now a sheriff's deputy. This accomplishment was the next step to becoming a police officer. I was not there yet, but I now had a foothold in the law enforcement profession. Oh, my salary was $9.00 an hour. Sometimes, dreams begin in the basement. However, I was just happy to be there.

My life was coming together. After years and years of meandering in shame, I was finally getting everything together. I was a late bloomer. With a beautiful wife, a son, another one on the way, a new home, and now a burgeoning career in law enforcement, I knew I was on my way!

Upon graduation from the Police Academy, I worked in the central jail, comprised of three thousand inmates who included murderers, rapists, bank robbers, gang members, and the rest of society's most refined. Of course, they were all *innocent*. Just go and ask them. They will tell you they got railroaded into prison. This initial look into "all things prison" allowed me to gain firsthand experience in each area of penitentiary detail. I was eager and excited to offer myself to this position. My father would be so proud of me. I never lost sight of my dream to get into law enforcement. After this exposure period, I was ready to be given an assignment.

My first position was a "kitchen deputy," which was a cake job for me. Did I mention it was the graveyard shift? Yes, that is right, I worked from 11:00 p.m. to 7:00 a.m. This duty would be my responsibility for the next twelve months. I sat on an elevated platform and supervised breakfast made by other inmates every morning as they prepared breakfast for several hundred inmates. If you call a bowl of oatmeal, two toast pieces, a powdered egg, and a piece of fruit a hearty breakfast, then welcome to prison life. Here is a warning to all wannabe criminals out there. Do not break the law! The terrible food will remind you that crime does not pay. Prison chow makes hospital meals look like the buffet at Caesar's Palace! If you like to eat and a great meal is essential to you, stay clean unless you think being herded into a mess hall at 5:00 a.m. every day is the joy of living.

Each morning, when the lieutenant would arrive for the day shift, we exchanged kind words and small talk. We built a working relationship during those brief moments. My hard work and effort paved the way for what career advances lay ahead. *My work ethic was getting noticed by those who managed the prison.* My lieutenant asked me if I wanted to continue learning my skills in law enforcement. Resoundingly, I said, "Yes, I do!" I was asked to become a juvenile drill instructor. Being accepted, I went to Fort McCullen, Alabama, for Drill Instruction School. This base was owned and operated by the United States Army. Yes, I served this time, much like a drill sergeant would approach Bootcamp for tactical training.

Although a condensed version for drill instructors for my needs, it was intense, mind-altering, and life-changing. Once again, I was one of the oldest members of the instructor team. I did not let that affect me or detour me. I kept my mind focused and my body healthy. Each day, I gave it my all and wanted to do my best in this preparation. When the instructor training was completed, I received the top honor graduate award among my peers. *Thankfully, I was now a full-time juvenile drill instructor.*

The drill instructor's role was a position that attempted to instill values and respect in young men and women. I directly impacted young people's lives, not just by mixing margaritas, hitting on women, or pushing term insurance.

I was making a difference!

I worked in the juvenile hall unit and fell in love with the young people there. I kept a healthy emotional distance, but I was like a dad or an uncle to a lot of them. They were nowhere near hardened criminals. These were young people who had lost their way. I could relate to them. I saw myself in them and all the shame that had held me back in their behaviors. They were good kids and needed direction for their futures. It was imperative to keep the relationship a professional one. It would have been easy to slip into a "friendship" with these teens, but I was hired to provide oversight and instruction for them, not be their buddy. Sadly, my peers did not keep these lines clearly defined and "mixed it up" with the juveniles. In one instance, I had to step up and report an improper relationship.

One of my fellow drill instructors used to play cards with the inmates and swap stories about their crime days. I reported him to our CO. We are not there to mingle but to maintain security. I took my job very seriously. On my days off, I was fun-loving and hung out with my friends. The people I supervised were never my pals. The drill instructor I reported to my supervisor was written up for "conduct unbecoming." He had put himself and his fellow drill instructors at risk by being sloppy. If he ever let his guard down, these savvy felons would have killed him in a heartbeat and any other deputy they saw.

While that was hard to do, it was the right thing to do. These "defining moment" decisions will be the setup for opportunities moving forward in life. Do the right thing, and you will get noticed. I promise you that. How do I know that to be true? Well, for starters, I continued to learn my craft as a law enforcement professional. Also, I continued to apply for police officer roles in my local area. I had to be patient and wait on God's timing.

Faithfully, I served in the role of drill instructor from 1996 to 1998, but my day in the sun was coming. I applied one more time for a police officer position. This time, it would be the Hollywood Police Department. As in times past, I put it before the Lord in prayer. Within a matter of weeks, I was chosen to become one of Hollywood's elite police officers. Can you believe it? *It had finally arrived.* My dream came true. I was humbled and blessed. God had come through in His timing. I knew that God had opened the door, and this time, I was ready for the mission. Let me give you some friendly advice:

Never give up on your dreams!

> *"Don't downgrade your dream just to fit your reality. Upgrade your conviction to match your destiny!"* -Lisa Burdette

The long road from my abusive home life to struggling financially and irresponsibly getting a girl pregnant was in my rearview mirror now. For some reason, the good Lord was smiling down at me, and I smiled back at Him. If you had a tough life growing up and continuously had to overcome setbacks, bad choices, and unfortunate circumstances, *do not give up*. If you struggled in school, lived irresponsibly, and were frequently laden with shame, loneliness, and people who never believed in you, *do not give up*. If it seemed like life had a way of chaining your dreams to the fire hydrant, here is my BEST advice for you, *do not give up!*

Be determined to win, despite how things look.

Never settle for mediocrity in life. Get up when life knocks you down. Keep on believing in yourself and giving it your all. Your day is coming. I promise you. I am a living example of God's grace and guidance. You must learn to trust God and listen to His leading. It pays off in the end. Trust me on this! I am the poster child for God, rewriting your story for a masterful outcome.

I was going to be a police officer.

Let us learn more in the next chapter together.

KEEPING IT REAL!

1. A Sheriff's Deputy . . . Are you willing to start small to fulfill your dreams?

2. Patience is never easy when we want something. Can you share how patience works in your life?

3. I related to the young people in prison. Can God use you to relate to others? How?

4. I found my power. How? Commit to memorize Philippians 4:13 (NKJV), "I can do all things through Christ who strengthens me." Can you relate?

5. **Press on!** "¹³ Brethren, I do not count myself to have apprehended; but one thing *I do,* forgetting those things which are behind and reaching forward to those things which are ahead, ¹⁴ **I press** toward the goal for the prize of the upward call of God in Christ Jesus" (Philippians 3:14–14 NKJV). ***How?***

~ Verse to Memorize ~

Wisdom calls aloud outside; She raises her voice in the open squares. -Proverbs 1:20 (NJKV)

11

MY DREAM LIFE CONTINUES

As I took the job at the Hollywood Police Department in Hollywood, Florida, I had to do cross-over training with my new employer. In other words, because I had already been to the Police Academy earlier and continued my learning as a drill instructor at Fort McCullen, a condensed program was all I needed to step into this new role as a police officer. I must say, as a law enforcement professional, I had found my passion, and this love had intercepted me. I became highly skilled and trained to be the best in my field and was decorated with awards and commendations, including Lifesaving, and many other awards. I received "Officer of the Month" several times and "Detective of the Month" on numerous occasions.

I was relentless in my mission to be the finest in every single area of police work. I was continually taking courses in SWAT Tactics, Officer Survival, and Field Training. I became a Forensic Artist and received advanced training from other law enforcement courses. *However, my favorite activity was being able to interact with people in the community.* I am a people person, and to make our citizens smile and feel safe brought pleasure to my soul every week! It was my daily inspiration.

Notwithstanding, I kept *adding* to my expertise. I joined the detective division as a burglary detective and was a street crimes detective working undercover in street crime activity. It was all exciting to train for such jobs. I was not too fond of this one part, and most of my fellow officers had to endure begrudgingly: *Bureaucracy. It was a vortex of emotion.*

The internal politics, which always led to bickering among police officers and their supervisors, negatively affected the entire department. Instead of having the patience and tolerance for the department infighting, I struggled to hold it together. I am a positive guy, and I want everyone to be happy around me. That was not happening here. As a sensitive man who hates arguing and pettiness, all these negatives proved to be too much for me.

While I enjoyed my free time getting away from the job, I never compromised my concentration and effectiveness of being a professional police officer. Being Stephen Lynch Harrison Sr., the man was comfortable for me. I liked being in great shape and using my various communication skills to talk to people, making them laugh and feel comfortable around me. People loved me, and I loved them.

Can I take a few minutes and give you some sound advice? Trust me, I don't want to sound preachy or pushy here, but simply live for an audience of ONE: Jesus Christ. Sure, I got plenty of awards for my service and I wanted to be the best at what I did every day. That is just how I was raised. Nonetheless, the awards will get put into the closet and over the years gather dust on them. Important now—yes! Not so much when you are in your golden years. Concurrently, you will always have "office politics" to deal with that steals the thunder out of your work setting. I get that too. People grumble. People are negative. Problems abound in any job environment. Don't let it get inside of your mind and heart.

Nevertheless, in light of Eternity, awards and politics will not matter one iota. You will stand before the Lord and He will ask you two questions. 1.) Do you know my Son, Jesus Christ, personally? 2.) What did you do, in this life, with the things entrusted to your care? Your wife, your children, your finances, etc. There is NO wiggle room around these two questions. No grading on a curve or hoping to tip the scales of good things over bad things. Look to the Cross for your validation. God settled your worth there as noted in John 3:16 (NIV), "For God so loved the world that He gave His one and only son that whosoever believes in Him shall not perish, but have eternal life." Enough said!

KEEPING IT REAL!

1. I poured myself into my dream. Would you be willing to give so much to yours?

2. Fast-paced living has a price tag. Do you live with such a pace? How has it impacted your life?

3. Why is it so easy to want to be awarded?

4. Putting on the happy face. Do you focus on your image more than honesty with yourself? Who are you trying to impress?

5. Right living. Does it matter? See the Word of God in Psalms 31:1 (NIV), "In you, LORD, I have taken refuge; let me never be put to shame; deliver me in your **righteousness**."

~ Verse to Memorize ~

[10] Choose my instruction instead of silver, knowledge rather than choice gold, [11] for wisdom is more precious than rubies, and nothing you desire can compare with her. -Proverbs 8:10–11 (NIV)

12

JUST THE FACTS, MA'AM

As mentioned, in 1998, I got hired by the Hollywood, Florida Police Department. It was a wonderful feeling. I was not just a policeman in my new career. I was the consummate professional. I was also as versatile as Dustin Hoffman with a script. I could play any character I got assigned to without breaking a sweat. I loved it.

Let me list the ways I served my community,

Burglary Detective
Undercover Cop
SWAT Officer
Patrol Officer
Community Liaison
Forensic Sketch Artist

Oh, the stories I could tell you. As a field training officer, I enjoyed working the streets and training new recruits. One day while I was training a new recruit, we received a Code 3 call which meant get there as fast as possible, about a burglary in progress in the neighborhood we were patrolling that day.

I cautioned my recruit to slow down, "Because this is a property crime, and the homeowner has homeowner insurance to cover the stolen goods, and there's no need to go 100 mph." This excessive speed would endanger everyone's life, including ours, for stolen property that will be reimbursed! It is not like he had a kid for ransom here.

When I arrived, to my surprise, the bravo shift officers were on the scene and requesting the crime scene unit to respond. I asked the officer on the scene if he cleared the house to ensure no one was inside. He said nobody was inside. I responded that the suspect was still in the house! Because I can hear him making noise inside the house. I yelled inside and said "We know you're inside!" and I had K9 responding. The next thing I knew, the suspect kicked the front door from the inside, striking the day sergeant at the front door in the face and knocking him to the ground.

The suspect then bolted out the door running across school property. I groaned, "Great, now we have a *lockdown* situation affecting 1,500 students, teachers, and staff. It keeps getting better and better!" He must have been a lousy student because he wanted no part of the campus. He bolted into one door and flew out of another as he headed for a neighborhood. I was going verbally crazy at this point, "This idiot is trying to break every law in a community within an hour. What was next, indecent exposure?"

We ended up losing him but received a tip that he was hiding out with some gang members in a nearby home. A few other officers and I responded to the house where we received the tip. Due to exigent circumstances, we entered the house to apprehend the suspect. Immediately I was confronted by two teenagers whose apparent goal in life was to mouth off to a cop, which they did. Boy, was that a "Big Mistake" for them! I grabbed the wannabe gang members and took them outside while my fellow officers carefully surrounded *Burglary Boy* inside the house and cut off all his options. This situation was going to be good.

While I was busy babysitting Beavis and Butthead, one of them slipped. To stop himself, he punched me in the face. I flattened him as an armadillo pounded by a Dr. Pepper truck on a Texas highway. Then, his buddy came at me and went down like a football receiver meeting Dick Butkus at the goal line. He did not see it coming. I laughed until I looked up at the sky and saw the local news helicopter recording the whole thing. You got to love the press. They are always meddling!

A few months later, I was being sued by the parents of the wannabe gang bangers in Federal Court for excessive police force. It was the judge's turn to be the Dr. Pepper truck. I won the case. Oh, by the way, the burglar wound up in prison. Life was sweet! Street patrol was never dull, and the acts of sheer stupidity were unending. Criminals are not the wisest people in the community. I learned a great deal about human nature.

What about the Street Crimes Unit? I logged time there as well. We were always busting prostitutes, gamblers, and drug dealers. The hookers were a sight for sure. I know that when times are tough, everyone must figure a way to survive, but these poor women were more like the Star Wars bar scene than Evelyn in *Pretty Woman*. Maybe they had been gorgeous beauties at a time in their lives. However, since most of them were drug addicts and continued living on the street, their flowers faded way too early in the day. Nevertheless, I felt sorry for them. I even felt sorry for some of their customers. One guy we busted was an FBI agent on the verge of retirement with a twenty-five-year pension. Had we arrested him, he would have lost it all. My boss said, "Let him walk away. It's a misdemeanor, and he put in a lot of time for his community. We're not going to ruin his life over an hour of pathetic pleasure." I agreed, and the cop got his pension. I felt right about that.

My time as an undercover cop was quite eventful as well. We were always chasing a suspect racing away from us. Just the facts! I remember one day, while on the job, I was in a terrible accident. Two people were killed. As for myself, I went headfirst into a windshield and almost joined them at the Pearly Gates, too. I would not have been typing this book if I had been in my assigned unmarked. But God had a plan of protection that day for me. My sergeant was going on vacation, and he told me I could use his SUV. Thank God! It was much a bigger and sturdier vehicle, and because of it saved my life.

Unfortunately, I developed a severe case of vertigo for six months. If you relish the feeling of dizziness when you step off the Mad Hatter Teacups at Disney World, then try it 24/7. You cannot think straight, and you cannot walk straight, and you would swear you are drunk. For half a year, I was stumbling around, and it was horrible. Yeah, I hit a few walls, literally. Thank God, it finally lifted, and I went from *Dazed and Confused* to *On a Clear Day, You Can See Forever!* I enjoyed the second movie better. Police work was not for the weary, I must say!

KEEPING IT REAL!

1. Why was I so passionate about my new career? Do you live your life with such passion?

2. Always learning more! Do you seek personal growth daily? Why or why not?

3. I almost died in that accident. Do you think about death? Are you ready to meet God?

4. Salvation = Surrender. Giving your heart to Jesus is about letting Him lead your life. Would you choose Him today?

5. Let these words sink in your soul. Ephesians 2:8–9 (NKJV), "⁸ For by grace you have been saved through faith, and that not of yourselves; *it is* the gift of God, ⁹ not of works, lest anyone should boast." Do you want God's gift?

~ Verse to Memorize ~

Give *instruction* to a wise *man,* and he will be still wiser;
Teach a just *man,* and he will increase in learning.
-Proverbs 9:9 (NKJV)

13

IN WALKS KEVIN

There was this guy, a cop named Kevin.

I met Kevin when I started my career on the force in 1998. I had heard he was a funny guy, likable and comical, from my fellow officers. Our professional connection did not become a reality when I was assigned to the road patrol, a place where all the rookies begin their careers. It was there that I got to know Kevin briefly. He would respond to calls as my backup, and I would do the same for him. In 2003, I was transferred to the detective bureau to work in the burglary unit, and because Kevin worked in the domestic violence unit, we would see each other more often, and of course, we got to know each other pretty well.

We were friends, primarily at work. I did not socialize with him or the people he hung out with because we didn't have much in common other than on the job. As I mentioned, Kevin was **a funny guy who enjoyed making everyone** laugh, and people loved him. He knew everyone and had dozens of friends on the force. The chief and all the command staff knew and tolerated him. He was a colorful guy, but one thing always stood out about him, as I recall. He was frequently *involved* in something, most likely for financial gain.

Kevin was a constant hustler. He was one of the guys who probably watched a lot of gangster movies growing up. He knew all those films by heart and could recite every line, from *The Godfather* to *Goodfellas* to *Casino*, you name it. Kevin knew those movies well and was a great impersonator of Brando, De Niro, and Pacino, to name a few. Kevin saw all of them! He also knew all the songs by Frank Sinatra. As I said, he was lively and amusing, too! So, it was easy to like Kevin. He was a moral person and would help anyone. He was a devoted husband and father and a faithful Catholic. Nevertheless, you always got the feeling that there was a catch whenever he did something for you, like, "I did you a favor, and you owe me," kind of thing.

Like Don Corleone.

In 2005, I took the sergeant's test and did well. I finished in the top five ahead of many guys who had master's degrees and PhDs. Not bad for a guy with only a little college experience! What was the secret to my success? *I loved being a cop!* To get promoted, I had to be reassigned back to patrol. That was the drill. I was transferred to Charlie Shift, 3:00 to 11:00 p.m. One night, I received a call from Kevin, and he asked me, "Steve, do you want to make some money on an off-duty detail? I asked him, "What's the job?" Kevin replied, "I have some friends coming in from New York that want to play some high-stakes poker. I was hoping you could help us organize the guests for an hour, and I will give you $100. Does that sound fair?" I said, "Okay, where's the detail?"

He filled me in on the work detail. Kevin said, "It's not in the city. It's in Fort Lauderdale at Pier 66." I thought to myself, *"Pier 66?"* I informed him, "Kevin, you know we cannot work an off-duty detail outside our city limits. We could get in trouble. It's against our policy." He assured me, "We will not be in uniform or using our police vehicles. We will be in a coat and tie and driving our vehicles. It is a private job. *There's nothing illegal here, Steve."* As a result, I agreed to do the detail.

I met Kevin in a hotel lobby, dressed in my suit as he had requested. He proceeded to tell me, "We need to go meet a friend of mine in one of the rooms. I said, "Who's we?" Then, I see Sergeant Jeff Courtney and Detective Thomas Simcox. Courtney was on the job for sixteen years and was currently assigned to the sex crimes division as a sergeant. Simcox was a seasoned officer of twenty-four years and had spent most of his career in vice and narcotics. He was currently assigned as a detective in the robbery division. At that point, I felt a little more at ease seeing these guys because they had been around the block and had excellent reputations. Little did I know that these guys had been involved in Kevin's criminal activities for some time now. I was suspicious of the activities ahead, but I went along with it just the same. *I trusted Kevin!*

We went to the room to meet Kevin's poker friends, Mikey, and Anthony, who, by the way, similarly happened to be undercover FBI agents. They were both very personable and likable. They proceeded to tell me that they had rented a yacht for their high-stakes poker game since it was illegal, and they had to play a certain distance out in the ocean to get around the law.

International waters.

My job was to sit in the parking lot with my lights on, and when anyone would approach my vehicle, a distinctive-looking big black Ford F-250 Crew Cab Four-Wheel Drive for directions to "Fredo's" birthday party, I was to give them the details. Fredo was the party name. REALLY, Kevin? Couldn't they come up with a better name than that? Then, I remembered how much Kevin loved *The Godfather* movie! For the next hour, I directed them, "Fredo Party" guests, to room 279 until I got a call from Kevin to meet him back at the room. When I arrived at the room, Kevin told me, "Mikey wants to give you something!" Mikey walked over and said, "Thanks for helping us out,

Stevie. We appreciate it!" Next, he reached out and placed some cash in my hand. I thanked him and quickly put it into my pocket without even looking at it.

When I got into my truck, I reached into my pocket and almost fainted! To my shock and surprise, it counted out as five $100 bills! I was speechless over that amount for one hour's work. I made all that money just by giving directions. That seemed generous of him, but I figured, "High-stakes poker guy!" As I headed home on that Saturday night, I called Dianne and told her, "Get dressed! We're going out to Longhorn's for dinner and then to the Roundup for a few drinks!" She asked me, "What's the occasion?" I laughed, "Because I just made $500 working a private detail for an hour!" She responded, "For only an HOUR?" I said, "Yep! Let us go out and have some fun!" We sure did.

KEEPING IT REAL!

1. Friends bring out the best or worst in us. Do you have a "Kevin" in your life?

2. I was always asking questions about the details. Do you think I knew something was up? How?

3. The Bible warns about sordid gain in Proverbs 1:14,19, "[14] Cast in your lot among us, Let us all have one purse," "[19] So *are* the ways of everyone who is greedy for gain; It takes away the life of its owners." **What can be learned here?**

4. "I trusted Kevin!" Do you trust <u>all</u> your friend's actions?

5. Memorize Luke 12:15 (NKJV), "And He (Jesus) said to them, 'Take heed and beware of covetousness, for one's life does not consist in the abundance of the things he possesses.'" Do you believe that?

~ Verse to Memorize ~

If you live wisely, you will live a long time;
wisdom will add years to your life. -Proverbs 9:11 (NCV)

14

LITTLE BY LITTLE

Two months after the rigged poker game, Kevin told me that his friends, Mikey and Anthony, were in town from New York and wanted him to see if he could hire a couple of guys to follow one of their truck drivers who was transporting cigarettes to another city. Supposedly, they were telling Kevin that their trucks were getting hijacked, and that is why they needed some security.

When Kevin approached me about helping him, my first instinct was to ask Kevin, *"What are we protecting?"* He told me, "Just cigarettes." I asked Kevin, "What do they want us to do if the truck *does* get hijacked because we're not in uniform or a marked police car." He said, "Just drive away." I pressed his lack of logic, "Why are we providing security to stop the truck from getting hijacked if we are not going to protect anything?" He just repeated himself, "Don't worry. If something happens, just drive away!"

His ridiculous comments should have been a *red flag* for me. *My instincts were right.* After I was arrested, I found out that the cigarettes were stolen, and the tractor-trailer was too!" The FBI had set this operation up from the beginning. They had posed as two guys who told Kevin (who absurdly believed he was the wisest guy around) that they needed a few guys to follow a stolen tractor-trailer. The truck had been stolen out of Miami from the Miccosukee Indian Reservation, which sold cigarettes to the public for less money, securing profits. Now, we have a stolen truck with stolen cigarettes, all cleverly set up by the FBI and slowly but surely moving Kevin and his gang to federal prison, including me, *the club's latest, clueless member.*

As usual, Kevin did not give me all the facts. As a result, I agreed to help him out again. Unbeknown to me, I am well on my way to securing a prison cell. Dutifully, I followed that truck with Tommy, and we tailed the rig for about ten miles to the designated exit. The plan was to meet Kevin at the Seminole Hard Rock Casino in Hollywood. I met with Kevin, Jeff, and Tommy, and we were all waiting to have dinner with Mickey and Anthony.

During dinner, Mickey tells Kevin, "Hey, I need to take Stevie upstairs because I want to talk to him!" Kevin nods his assent and tells me, "Go upstairs with Mickey. He wants to talk to you." I go with Mickey, and when we arrive at the room, he thanks me for helping him out with the truck. He fails to mention that it was stolen along with the contents inside. Next, he pulls a large sum of money out of the bag and begins to count out twenty-five $100 bills, and asks me to verify the amount. When I do, he says to me, "This is for you." I was puzzled.

My first response was to say, "Thank you, but you don't have to give me anything. I didn't do anything other than follow a truck for a few miles, plus you are a friend of Kevin's, so I don't mind helping you out." He insisted I take the money, and we went back and forth arguing about it until I finally said, "Okay." Little did I know that the room was wired for video and sound. That is why Mikey wanted me to take the cash. The feds now had more dirt on me. Of course, they did. *Now, it would be just a matter of time.*

KEEPING IT REAL!

1. *Little by Little!* Is it easy to justify wrongdoing? Why?
2. Red Flags? Does God give us signs to warn us of future harm? How?
3. Have you ever ignored a "Red Flag" in your life? What was the outcome?
4. **Pride can be your downfall.** What does God say about it? "Likewise, you younger people, submit yourselves to *your* elders. Yes, all of *you* be submissive to one another and be clothed with humility, for God resists the proud, But gives grace to the humble" (1 Peter 5:5 NKJV). *Are you humble? How?*
5. We all think, "That could never be me!" How are you protecting your soul against corruption?

~ Verse to Memorize ~

Treasures of wickedness profit nothing, but righteousness delivers from death. *The blessing of the* LORD *makes one rich, And He adds no sorrow with it.* -Proverbs 10:2, 22 (NKJV)

15

GOING FROM BAD TO WORSE

It had been a month since the cigarette job. I got a phone call from Kevin, and he asked me if I wanted to have lunch. He told me to meet him at the Diplomat Hotel on the beach, a famous Hollywood hangout. Over lunch, he proceeded to say to me, "I need to pick up one of my friends, a guy named Bobby, and take him to the airport. He is waiting for me in his hotel room."

We arrive at the room, and Kevin introduced me to Bobby. Next, they go into another room to talk privately. I overheard Bobby ask him, "So, is this guy Stephen good?" Kevin responds, "Yeah, he's a good guy." They return to the room, and Bobby opens a small suitcase, and inside are three little pictures of artwork. He puts on latex gloves and shows Kevin the artwork. Then, I overheard Bobby whisper to Kevin, "This art is stolen." One of Chucky's bookies owed him and Bobby a lot of money from an outstanding gambling debt. He was using the fenced artwork to pay them back instead of cash. *I was watching a crime in progress, but I could not say a thing as I was there, as well.* My comfort level was quickly getting challenged.

Finally, Bobby puts the artwork back into the suitcase, and he and Kevin head to the airport. *I was not happy with Kevin for leaving out essential details and inviting me to an "innocent" lunch.* He had a severe agenda here. It was, at least shady, and most likely, criminal. After

Kevin put Bobby on the plane, Kevin asked me to accompany him later in the week to Atlantic City to drop off the artwork. I said, "No." I told him, "I cannot get off work." He laughed, "Do not worry, I can arrange that for you!" Then, I said, "I do not have any money for the trip." Again, he assured me, "Do not worry about that, either!"

Kevin was acting like a wise guy, the kind you see in the film *Goodfellas. I was being sucked into his web.* Worse yet, we were being watched by the feds. Little did I know my future was being jeopardized. Kevin was becoming terrible news. *I needed to end this relationship sooner than later.* I reluctantly agreed to go. We got to Atlantic City and checked into a hotel room, and he said, "We're waiting for a phone call." I felt uneasy if I were candid. Something did not feel right in my gut!

Later in the day, Kevin got the call and received information that his friend, Bobby, wanted to come up to the room and drop off the suitcase. He brought along a friend, Anthony, who I remembered from the poker game. Additionally, a second guy, an older man whom I had never seen before, came as well. He was an older man in his fifties and looked like a mafia-type. I was making new friends left and right, thanks to Kevin.

Kevin and I were sitting in two chairs facing Bobby and Anthony. The old guy was sitting to the right of us overseeing things. It was creepy. Bobby and the older man gave Kevin $7,000, and next they gave me $3,000 and said, "This is for you!" Yes, I was becoming "one of the guys!" Unfortunately, I did not use enough caution here. I protested, "You do not need to give me this. I just came along for the ride!" But, of course, they did. They needed me to take the money to use me for more of their activities until I was too deep to walk away. That is how corruption works. I was digging a giant hole for myself here.

I agreed to take the money even though I was not sure why they were giving it to me at the time. I was now swimming with sharks, and I was going to be eaten alive. Nevertheless, I took the money. We all

67

went out to dinner. It was Kevin and his band of merry gangsters aka "FBI agents." We had a great time together. The next day, since I had never been to Atlantic City, Kevin insisted that he show me around.

Of course, he took me to some famous ITALIAN restaurant on the boardwalk called Carmines. The food was excellent. I think I saw Fredo there. Also, we did a little shopping for our wives. We went into the Coach store, and I bought Dianne a couple of purses. The next day we flew home. I had no idea that Kevin's friends paid the airfare. I should have known better, but the money was a nice perk. *I was slowly losing my integrity and my convictions.* Money has a way of blinding your eyes to the truth. Your desired lifestyle will cause you to compromise. I sure did. *I never thought I would end up there.*

After the trip to Atlantic City, I did not hear much from Kevin for a few months. Everything was quiet. Little did I know that the FBI was setting up one final deal to put the nail in the coffin causing the death of the other guys and me. Kevin's friends, aka FBI agents, were still in touch with him daily. One day I got a call from Kevin while I was working patrol to meet him somewhere. He needed to talk to me about something. Quickly, I arranged to meet with Kevin, and we were cutting up like old times. It felt good. Then, he told me that his friends were coming into town and wanted our help protecting a shipment of merchandise from Home Depot. Kevin said his "friends" were concerned about their truck being highjacked because some of them were getting highjacked, lately. They simply wanted our help for their merchandise. At that moment, I began to question him about his relationship with his friends. I wanted to know how he had met them, and how long they'd known each other. That was a fair question given the nature of this last assignment. Things just didn't add up for me. Kevin was quick to calm me, "Stevie, I told you that I have known them for a few years, and they were my friends from New York where I grew up. Relax!" Then, I said, "Kevin, keep it real with me and don't bullsh*t me." Next, I asked him, "What is going to be in this truck? Is it drugs or guns?" He laughed and said, "I would never get you involved in something like this. We have families and our careers, and you are getting ready to be promoted to sergeant." I told Kevin, "Don't BS me because if it's guns or drugs. Then, I am out of here right now." As I started to walk away, Kevin said, "Stevie, I am telling you the truth. I would never do something to get you into trouble because you're a good man." I should have known he was lying through his teeth and using me to facilitate his greed all the more. Several weeks passed, and eventually, Kevin reached out to let me know the date and time we would be helping his friends out.

Two weeks before I would follow the tractor-trailer coming from the back of Home Depot, I learned that Kevin was down in Miami at the Ritz Carlton Hotel, discussing the plan with his so-called friends/ aka FBI agents. Little did I know Kevin had a different plan than the one he told me several weeks before. This "new" plan was for him, Jeff, and Tommy to follow a truck from Miami to Hollywood, Florida supposedly carrying a few kilos of heroin. That's right, HEROIN! What happened to following a tractor-trailer coming out of the back of Home Depot? I guess Kevin didn't want me to know about the new plan.

I wondered why. Well, I will tell you why! I didn't find this out till I was in prison. One day I was meeting with my prison counselor, and she wanted me to review my case file which outlines my criminal case. While checking my file, I noticed a document recording Kevin discussing the plan at the Ritz Carlton Hotel. Sadly, he never knew that this was being recorded and recorded like all the other so-called off-duty details I was working on.

At that time, the friends/FBI agents asked Kevin if everyone knew what they would be protecting in the tractor-trailer. Kevin responded that everyone knew except Stevie. The friends/FBI agents said, "What do you mean he doesn't know?" Everyone needs to know the contents, in case the feds are involved. That should have been a red flag for Kevin when they mentioned, "in case the feds were involved!" Nevertheless,

Kevin said, "If I tell Stevie the truth, he won't do the assignment." The friends/FBI agents were persistent in ensuring Kevin told me before the detail took place. Guess what? Kevin never told me because he knew that I would never be a part of something like this. Do you want to guess when I found out what was really in the truck? How about when I returned to the Ritz Carlton Hotel suite with Kevin, Jeff, Tommy, and Kevin's so-called friends/FBI agents, the place they were staying? We were all in the suite as the conversations were happening. Remember as I said before, everything was being video and audio recorded.

I remember sitting in one of the chairs in the room, and there were several other guys I had never seen or met before. I recognized Mikey and Anthony, whom I met with Kevin when I worked the birthday party detail. Instantly, I felt in my spirit, right from the beginning, that something wasn't right here. Now, while I was sitting there hearing everyone talking about drugs and jewelry, I discerned that I was in deep trouble. At that very moment, I just sat there in shock, listening to everyone's conversation, waiting to get out of the room and this situation. I noticed Kevin entered one of the bedrooms because it was a suite. Next, I noticed Jeff went in and came out, and then finally, Tommy went in and came out as well. Lastly, I heard Kevin say, "Stevie, come here." I got up and proceeded to walk into the back bedroom. As I walked in, I met the Big Guy, Big Jack.

This was the first time I had ever heard his name or met him. However, he looks the part of a Wise Guy, or should I say, the Big Boss. He was about six-two, three hundred pounds, heavy set with slicked-back, black hair, wearing a diamond Rolex watch, several gold chains, and a black guayabera shirt. Oh, I forgot to mention that his name was Jack Falcone, a decorated FBI agent, who had worked on some of the most prominent organized crime cases. He was legendary!

As I entered the room, Big Jack introduced himself and said, "I've never had the pleasure of meeting you, Stevie." I am Big Jack! Well, he fits the part, that's for sure, especially when you're three hundred pounds. He then proceeds to thank me for helping them out. Next, he said, "This is something we usually don't do." He went on to say, "Did Kevin tell you what was in the truck?" With a bit of concern and a little frustration, I said, "No." Big Jack spoke next and said, "Well, it wasn't jewelry! It was five or six pieces of heroin."

Before that actual statement, I did not know what was in the truck. But now I knew. I sure did! He said, "You don't have a problem with that, do you?" Are you kidding me? What was I supposed to say, at that moment? Can you imagine me saying, "Big Jack, yeah, I got a problem with that." I probably wouldn't have made it home that night if I had said that. Because I thought these guys were mafia guys, and they kill police officers too, I knew I was in deep trouble. In my mind, I just wanted to get out of there.

Big Jack thanked me again and then handed me $3,000. Finally, he wished me happy holidays. Little did I know I would be spending a lot of my holidays in federal prison. After the meeting, we all went downstairs to have dinner. As we were finishing dinner, everyone talked about wanting to go out to a few nightclubs. Tommy, one of the guys I worked with in the detective division, said he had to pass and needed to get home to his family. I said, "Yeah, I will pass because I needed to get home to my family, also." I ask Tommy to drive me back to my car. He said, "Sure, no problem."

When I got downstairs, I laid into Tommy and said, "You guys lied to me about what we were protecting and what was in the truck!" He said, "No, it was Kevin who lied to you because you wouldn't have come on board if he had told you the true contents." I was so mad that I didn't say a word all the way home. When I got to my car, I told Tommy, "Don't you or Kevin or Jeff ever call me or talk to me again!"

1 Timothy 6:10 (NKJV) says, "For the love of money is the root of all kinds of evil. And some craving for money have wandered from the true faith and pierced themselves with many sorrows."

The love of money blinded Kevin and the other guys. I know you are wondering what about me. Truthfully, I was not in it for the money. When you engage in criminal activities, you must have the intent for a crime to be committed. For example, when you commonly participate in a drug deal, you will be paid a predetermined amount for your involvement. Kevin never told me how much money I was going to make. I figured I would get paid like working on many of the other off-duty details I had worked on. I never intended to be involved in any illegal activity and I honestly believed I was working an off-duty detail as I have done before. You must be saying, "How naive you must be." Yes, I was naive and stupid to believe Kevin was telling the truth. No doubt, I was deceived many times by Kevin.

KEEPING IT REAL!

1. *Cash vs. Conviction.* Can one be bought if enough money is involved? Why?

2. **Greed is a killer.** Look at God's Word in 1 Timothy 6:9 (NKJV), "But those who desire to be **rich** fall into temptation and a snare, and *into* many foolish and harmful lusts which <u>drown</u> men in destruction and perdition." *Are you drowning?*

3. *Do you "love" money, more?* God warns in 1 Timothy 6:10 (NKJV), "**For the love of money** is a root of all *kinds of* evil, for which some have *strayed from the faith* in their greediness and pierced themselves through with many sorrows."

4. You pick. "[11] But you, O man of God, **flee** these things and *pursue* righteousness, godliness, faith, love, patience, gentleness" (1 Timothy 6:11 NKJV). *It is your choice.*

~ Verse to Memorize ~

Those who trust in their riches will fall, but the righteous will thrive like a green leaf. -Proverbs 11:28 (NIV)

16

BUSTED

Crime, in any form, is like pulling the pin on a grenade. Eventually, you know it will explode, yet you race against the time you have before everything gets destroyed. That is how I felt as I got deeper into the web of my involvement with Kevin. Like anything shady, it will eventually catch up with you. That was true for me as well. Let us do a flashback to that moment in time.

It was Feb 21, 2007, the day I was arrested. I remember that day like it was yesterday. I was at the gym in Weston, Florida, with my friend, Jim. He was my sergeant while I worked in street crimes. Jim was currently working on a new assignment as the department's K-9 Sergeant. While we were working out, I heard over the loudspeaker, "Steve Harrison, can you come to the front desk? You have a phone call."

Immediately, I went to the front desk to inquire. The girl at the desk said, "Steve, you have a phone call." Without haste, I picked up the phone and said "Hello." The person, on the other end, said, "Steve, this is Major Jones." Major Jones oversaw the detective's division that I used to work for a year earlier. I recognized his voice.

It should be noted that he was also my friend. He said, "Stevie, that's what some guys called me. I have bad news." At first, I thought maybe someone in my family was hurt or was killed. Then, I heard the words, "Stephen, you're going to be arrested today by the FBI." I thought this was someone playing a joke on me. I shot back, as I said, "Who is this, again?" He says, "Stevie, it's Major Jones." I said, "Major Jimmy Jones?" He repeated himself, "Yes, it is me, Jimmy." To catch my breath, I said, "Let me get your phone number, and I will call you right back."

Notwithstanding, he proceeds to give me his phone number. When I hung up the phone to dial the number, I saw the number was Jimmy's number. It was at that moment that I realized my life as I knew it was over. I had sensed for months that something was brewing, but this confirmed my suspicion, now.

I was in a fog.

I waited a few minutes to gather my thoughts and to get myself together. I thought to myself, "This must be a bad dream." I called back the number, and the person on the other end said, "Stevie, this is Major Jones, and I am sorry to have to give you this news. Today, you are going to be arrested by the FBI." I said back to him, "Can you tell me for what reason?" Major Jones replied, "I cannot give you that information other than what I am telling you." He went on to say, "The reason for my call is that the FBI agreed to allow us to come to pick you up and take you to the FBI headquarters in Miami, so they do not have to come to your house and kick the door down and scare your wife and your boys."

Major Jones continued to say, "Kevin Companion and Jeff Courtney have already been arrested, and Tommy Simcox is going to be turning himself in." Finally, Major Jones asked me if I would meet him at my house. Reluctantly, I said, "Yes, I will be there." Major Jones confirmed that he would pick me up along with Captain Sanchez. He went on to say that he needed my badge, guns, identification, and the keys to my car. While still a little stunned, I told him that I was on my way home. After I hung up the phone, my cell phone started ringing off the hook. Everyone was calling me as I guess somehow the word must have gotten out in the Hollywood Police Department.

You get to see your real friends in your times of trouble. It was nice to know that I had made some true-blue friends in my lifetime. *Take just a few minutes and put yourself in my shoes. What would be going through your head?* As for me, I was in utter disbelief. I could not breathe. I did not have anything to say right at this moment and time.

The next call was going to be the hardest. It was from my concerned and dear wife, Dianne. Awkwardly, I answered the phone. As expected, she was crying uncontrollably and asking me, "Stephen, what is going on?" She then said, "Stephen, everyone is calling me, asking where you are and if you are in trouble?" I reassured her, "No matter what happens, I love you." Dianne then asked, "Where are you?" I said, "I am on my way home with Jimmy from the gym. Do not worry or cry. Everything is going to be okay."

That was easy for me to say, but little did I know what lay ahead. Only God knew my unfolding future. If I were honest with myself, everything was going to have a life-changing effect on me. However, my wife, my two sons, family, and friends would be impacted for years to come. Yes, deep down in my soul, I knew everything was not going to be okay. My life that I knew that day would never be the same for my wife, Dianne, or my two sons, Stephen Jr. and Justin.

As I walked back from the front desk to where Jimmy was still working out, he could see in my countenance that something was desperately wrong. I guess it was because I looked like Casper, the Friendly Ghost. As I approached him, he said, "What's wrong, brother?" I said, "Jim, I am in a lot of trouble, and I am going to be arrested today by the FBI." He said, "What!" I said, "Yes, I am going to be arrested by the FBI" I, then, said, "I need you to take me home now." He said, "What the heck is going on here." I said, "Kevin Companion got me into trouble." He said, "How did Kevin get you into trouble?"

When we walked outside to get into his truck, I began to share some of the things I had done with Kevin. I told him that Kevin had asked me if I wanted to work some off-duty details, and I shared some of the off-duty details with my sergeant and good friend, Jimmy. When I told him the specifics, he said, "Why the heck did you get yourself involved with Kevin? He is bad news!" The things that I shared with him I honestly did not believe were criminal activity. To my surprise, the FBI thought quite differently than I did.

As I began to try to explain to him, he said, "What in the heck were you thinking?" I said, "I trusted Kevin!" My friend, Jimmy, said, "Stephen, that was your first mistake because he is a piece of s&#t that uses people for his purposes." He was shocked and pissed off at me. Jimmy said, "Steve, you are smarter than this, and you should have known something wasn't right!" I retorted back, "This is what Kevin told me, and I believed him!"

We were driving towards my house, only just minutes away, and my wife was calling me nonstop along with everyone else. All I could think of was that my life is over as I know it today. I pulled up in the driveway of my house. My wife came running up to me. As she was crying, she said, "What is going on? Why are you being arrested?" As I looked her in the eyes to tell her that everything was going to be alright, I saw my oldest son, Stephen Jr., age twelve, and my youngest son, Justin, age six, standing outside, crying and saying, "Daddy, What's going on?" It broke me inside!

I knew I had to be resilient because they have always seen me like the rock of our family, and I couldn't let them see me weak now. I looked at them both, along with their mother, and said, "Everything is going to be alright. Please don't cry." Deep within, I knew that nothing would be okay, and the life they knew was about to be torn away from them because of my poor decisions.

While I was still outside, Major Jones and Captain Sanchez pulled up in the driveway. Both expressed their sadness to me that they had to ask me for my gun and my badge. *Everything that I believed in and stood for was taken away in the blink of an eye, especially my integrity.* When you lose that, it's tough even to get it back again. You are now labeled a "convicted felon" and a "dirty cop." It shattered my heart into pieces.

I gave it my everything, each day, to serve and protect the citizens of Hollywood, Florida. Now, all the awards and honors for serving as an officer would mean nothing. Next, I gathered myself together, hugged my wife and sons, then told them, "I will be back." Yet, in my soul, I knew I was not coming right back. I was a nervous wreck and scared as could be as I got into the police car to be taken to the FBI headquarters in Miami.

I was sitting in the front seat of the SVR that they used to pick me up. Major Jones was driving while Captain Sanchez was sitting in the back seat behind me. As we drove, all I could think about was my family and the impact that my decisions were going to have on their lives. While we were driving, Major Jones said, "Let me give you some advice. No matter when you get there, do not say anything to the FBI until you have your lawyer present." I assured him that I would not do such and thanked him for his concern. I told both how sorry I was for what had happened. I was saddened to shame the chief and our department. It grieved me that I hurt the men and women who served there in Hollywood, Florida.

To my surprise, they both said, "Steve, you are a good person and what is happening to you is only because of Kevin. He lied and used you for his selfish purposes." At that moment, I started to break down crying as we talked and asked them to please make sure my family was alright. They both agreed that they would do so.

When we arrived at the FBI headquarters, we were greeted by a few agents dressed in their green BDUs which their SWAT team members wear. I felt as though I was a murder suspect by the way they all surrounded me. While I was being led inside, I could see all the local news helicopters flying overhead. I guess this was now breaking news, and everyone would know. Once inside, I was asked to take all my clothes off. I cannot even tell you how humiliating that was to be strip-searched, standing there naked in front of these people. Nonetheless, they were doing their job. When that was done, I was photographed and fingerprinted and then allowed to get dressed.

I was handcuffed a second time. This time was behind my back when one of the agents told the other agent to put the handcuffs in the front because I had a recent shoulder injury. I was taken aback by that simple gesture of kindness on their part. Next, I was brought into the interview room and was waiting to see who would be coming through the door to talk to me. Again, my brain was swirling with great concern.

It was a long wait, but eventually, two FBI agents came in to speak with me. After they made their introductions, they read me my Miranda rights. The agents said, "Steve, we are sorry, but unfortunately, you got caught up in the tail end of a two-and-a-half-year investigation on Kevin that was coming to a close." They went on to say, "Steve, we know are you not like the other guys." Curious, I asked them, "What do you mean by that?" I am sitting here arrested for something I do not even know what I did. They said they have been watching me for the last few months.

We know where you went to church and that you were a football coach for your son's team. We were at your charity boxing event at the Hard Rock where you were boxing. You are not like the other guys. Unfortunately, we know that you got dragged into this by Kevin Companion lying to you. You are an honest police officer, but you are held to a higher standard. They said, "We want to help you." I said, "What are you asking me to do?" Of course, I will tell the truth. But, they wanted me to make up things that did not happen, and I was not going lie and make up something about someone else and destroy that person's life and their family to save myself. *I was not made like that.*

I said, "I can only tell you what I was told and what I did." When they asked me if I wanted a lawyer, I said, "I would be more than happy to speak to you, but I needed to talk to my attorney first." They said, "We respect that, and we want to help in any way possible." They said, "Sit tight, and we will be transporting you and the other guys to the Federal Detention Center in Miami to be processed." About one hour later, they came in and told me that they needed to put some shackles and chains on me. My whole body was now one big shackle. They loaded us up in the FBI van and transported us to the Federal Detention Center in Miami, Florida.

Now, let me just share, from my heart, about my arrest. My world was shattered into a million pieces that day. In my mind, a thousand thoughts were running through my head. I had a wife and two children, for goodness sake. I cannot go to jail. Who will provide for my most significant asset, my family? That was my job. It was my honor and responsibility.

Sadly, if I were truthful about everything, we did not need the extra cash. I know what you are thinking, "Everyone can use more money for a rainy day." I get all that. Nevertheless, I had never spent the money I acquired. I had stashed it away, and when the legal proceedings started, I gave the entire sum of money back to the FBI agents. I know that is water under the bridge at this point in the whole outcome, but I felt better knowing that I did not squander the money on my private interests and lifestyle.

Next, we were taken up to the eleventh floor at the FBI headquarters, where all the high-profile criminals go. President Manuel Noriega was up there along with the Broward County Sheriff, Ken Jennings. As we arrive on the eleventh floor, all you can hear is screaming and yelling back and forth by all the other inmates. We all heard, "We got the police in the house." Then, all hell broke loose. Every cuss word known to man was now being hurled at us by the inmates on the floor.

It was safe to say that criminals do not like the police. Kevin and Jeff were placed together in a cell. I was placed in another one all by myself. If you're claustrophobic, like I am, you will not like the 10 x 6 cell footprint and sleeping on a metal bed with cockroaches running all over the place. What did I expect, the Trump Towers or a Hilton resort? In any event, if you want reasonable accommodations in life, do not break the law.

Once inside the cell, the guard told me to get some sleep because I will be getting up in a few hours to meet the federal magistrate judge. I said to myself, "Sleep, are you kidding me?" All I could think about was crying out to God. I keep asking Him for His forgiveness. I needed Him to be with my wife and sons as I might not be coming home. My need for sleep was not my most significant concern at the moment. I desperately needed God.

Nevertheless, I tried to get some sleep! Well, at least, I thought about doing it. Before I knew it, the guard was told to get me up and get me ready for court. They opened a little metal door where they gave me my food and told me to turn around to handcuff me. At once, I was wholly shackled and chained again. I felt like a sheep being led to the slaughter. Every emotion came crashing down on me. I tried to keep my composure, but it was hard to fathom what lay ahead. I truly needed God to give me grace for this moment.

I will never forget what happened next. As I entered the courtroom, I saw my father, who was dying of colon cancer, my mother, and my wife Dianne. They were all crying as they saw me enter the courtroom, shackled like a fugitive. I must be honest, here. It broke my heart to know the pain that I was causing those I loved for the poor decisions I had made. It was now my turn to stand before the judge and enter my plea of not guilty. In my heart, I was not guilty because Kevin had lied to me about the off-duty assignments. Several months later, little did I know that God would begin to show me who I was on the inside. After entering my not-guilty plea, the judge set my bond.

I was genuinely grateful and utterly shocked to hear that the prosecutor recommended to the judge that my bond be set to only $50,000. I was thankful for this reasonable amount. It was unusual considering that Kevin, Jeff, and Tommy's bonds were set at $250,000. Now that I look back on it and know what I know today, *only God could have orchestrated that outcome.* His Mercy is everlasting, even in the face of any difficulty. I left the courthouse and was placed in another holding cell till my bond was paid. To my surprise, my father and mother placed their home up as collateral. It just goes to show you that parents will do anything they can for their children. That is what love does. I was grateful for their love and concern for me during this time.

Once my bond was paid, I was free to go. I did not have any regular clothes. Thus, I had to wear the khaki brown prison uniform while leaving the courthouse. My attorney, who was hired to represent me for the first hearing, said, "There are a lot of news reporters waiting outside to get a picture of you and get you to say something." With that, we proceeded to exit out the back of the courthouse so we would not be seen. As I started to walk out, my attorney took off his suit jacket and told me to put it on.

It worked well. At least I thought it did until the reporters figured it out that I was wearing a blue sports coat with brown khaki prison pants. They, then, saw me start to walk hurriedly. It was kind of funny to see all the reporters running after me to get the story. Yet, I made my escape for the time being. Nonetheless, I knew not what lay ahead for me in the upcoming days. Did I tell you that I would be facing forty years to life? I really was!

After that, we went to the bail bondsman's office, which was right around the courthouse corner. There, I was told the requirements of my bond and the terms and conditions. If I failed to meet those requirements, I would lose the $15,000 that my father posted along with his house. At that moment, the *Shadow of Shame* came upon me with guilt and depression. I was facing going to prison for life! Let that sink in for a moment. As we were driving to my parent's house, a spirit of depression came upon me, saying, "Take your life." I remember when we pulled into the driveway of my parents, my wife and I continued sitting in the car to chat. I told her, "Dianne, I am not going to prison for the rest of my life." I went on to say, "I would rather take my life than spend the rest of my natural life in prison."

With that, I began to cry, and my wife started crying too. I said to her, "I am sorry for what I did. I do not want you and our sons to suffer for my decisions. If I get sentenced to life in prison, I am going to take my life." Then, I asked Dianne, "You must promise me you will help me end my life!"

The crazy thing is that my wife agreed to help me because she could not bear to see me in my current state of mind. Satan, who is the father of all lies, was desperately trying to take me out. He was on a mission to steal, kill, and destroy. However, God had a different plan for my life. My Heavenly Father said, *"Not today, Satan! I am about to do a completely new thing in my Son, Stephen's life. He does not even perceive it yet, but it has already begun."*

The next day was quite sobering as I began to look for a criminal attorney. It was my first order of business. As you would expect, they are not cheap! The talented ones are ridiculously priced. I am talking in the neighborhood of $250,000 to represent your case. I had no idea that my legal fees would topple $100,000 before the final sentence was rendered. Where did I have $100,000, you may be wondering? It was earned by me doing my extra police details over the years.

Yes, that was earned money by hard work and lots of it. I was remiss in giving it away for lawyer's fees. However, to save my hide from prison, I would gladly empty all my bank accounts. Here is some criminal math for you. In all my dealings, I only got $12,000 for my involvement. Now, I would find myself having to shell out over $100,000 to defend my case. Even when I was sentenced to 108 months in federal prison, I still had to make good on the lawyer's expenses. I know you heard that "crime does not pay," but trust me, I had to pay a lot in the end.

Also, I began to reach out to several friends in the law enforcement community for support. Finding an excellent criminal attorney was not easy. The first one we met with was a high-profile criminal defense attorney and a very high retainer fee to start reviewing my case. It was safe to say he was not the right one as I could not afford him. We continued our search. The following attorney was very friendly, and he had much experience with federal cases.

I was frustrated and depressed because I did not know what to do. My wife was so optimistic as she said, "We are going to find someone to help us," but she had no clue what was in front of me. With all federal cases, 97 percent of them plead out before going to trial. Why is that, you may wonder? I will tell you why. If you go to court against the Government of the United States of America along with the FBI, you're going to lose your case. Many defendants take a plea deal agreement even if they are not guilty to eliminate the courtroom need.

Let me make sure you understand that, so I will repeat it. "Even if you are not guilty and you go to trial to prove your innocence, the judges and the prosecutors believe you have wasted the court's time. As a result, they throw the book at you just for the sake of principle. I knew someone whom the government offered an eighteen-month sentence. *He was not even guilty, and he would not take a plea deal because he had not done anything wrong.* Well, just for taking his case to trial, the judge gives him seventeen years in prison. Yes, I said a total of seventeen years in federal prison. The federal justice system is broken, and first-time non-violent offenders are getting more time than someone in the state system accused of rape or murder. It is not right!

As God worked behind the scenes as He always does, I finally found a lawyer to represent my case. In my first few days out on bond, we got a call from a friend named Dan, a personal injury attorney. He told us that he had a friend who was a very respected federal criminal defense attorney by the name of Ed O'Donnell. Mr. O'Donnell agreed to meet with me at his office in the morning, and I briefly told him about my situation over the phone. We thanked him for his time and told him we would be there tomorrow bright and early.

The following day, we met with Mr. O'Donnell. He was an older gentleman and very distinguished-looking. He was with his son, Ed Jr., and we were pleased to be there. He began sharing with us a little about his background and his experience with cases like mine. He also told us his wife was a judge. I thought to myself, "Well, that's good because you know that judges, prosecutors, and lawyers all work together." In the end, it did not matter as the judge did his own thing.

Next, Mr. O'Donnell proceeded to ask me about my involvement, and I told him the truth. I am sure that all his clients say to him that they are "not guilty." However, I was not guilty other than being stupid and trusting someone who worked within my department. Nevertheless, I began to explain everything in full detail about what I did. He said that because this is a conspiracy case, I would do some jail time, but it wasn't going to be forty years to life. I said, "Are you sure about that?" He said, "Yes, I am." I cannot tell you how thankful I was to hear those words, but I now knew I was going to spend some time in jail. Let that sink in for a minute as you read this book. I was headed to the Big House. Nevertheless, I express gratitude to God, under my breath, as it was not for life. Thank God for small favors. At least, He heard my prayers. There would be a departure date down the road.

Mr. O'Donnell then proceeded to get to the main point, the money for fees! "How much money can you come up with?" he said rather confidently. I should have been quick to listen and slow to speak when he asked me that question. I looked him in the eye and said, "We have around $100,000 saved, and we could sell our house and give you the equity in it." He said, "No, you don't need to sell your house, but to get started, I will need $25,000 today to begin." Honestly, before that, we were praying to God to help us find someone, and my wife and I felt this was from God. We hired Mr. O'Donnell that day and wrote the check for $25,000. I admit that was hard to do, and it marked my heart.

Nonetheless, it is incredible when you think someone was sent into your path from God to help you. What I should have done was say, "Let me pray about it, and I will get back to you later in the week." Today, I would do that because God's wisdom is what leads me and directs my life. Nevertheless, that is today, but it was not that day. At that point, the process began, including the stress, depression, and the Shadow of Shame.

For the next few days, I tried to relax and gather my thoughts, but they were all over the place. Now, I know my attorney was telling me that I was going to do some time in prison. Yet, all the newspapers were saying the Hollywood officers would face life in prison, if convicted. If you were in my shoes, you probably would have felt the same as I did. A week shot by, and my attorney contacted me to tell me that we needed to meet with the FBI agents and the federal prosecutor assigned to my case in Miami.

We arrived at the FBI headquarters in Miami, and it was like Fort Knox. We went through every type of metal detector known to man. Once inside, we were escorted to a conference room. After a short wait, the two agents and the prosecutor entered the room. It was the first time seeing the agents again since my arrest and would be the first time to meet the prosecutor. Of course, after the introductions, they went right to work and started to ask me all kinds of questions about what I knew and who else was involved. I could tell that they were fishing for more knowledge because they felt more officers were participating and wanted to make more arrests.

After answering all these questions and listening to what they were saying, I realized they wanted me to take down other officers. I told them, "What are you saying and what you are asking me to make up was not true about other officers." They said, "You need to help yourself out and let us know what else you are not telling us. We can help you." It was right then when I said, "Gentlemen, you asking me to lie and make up things on these other officers that are not accurate. I cannot, and I will not do that. All I can tell you is what I did and what Kevin told me." I would not destroy other officers and their family's lives to save myself because I was not raised like that. As hard as it was to swallow, I would only accept responsibility for the poor decisions I made.

After which, they said, "We are not asking you to lie, but only tell the truth." Great, I said, "I cannot speak for anyone else other than my involvement." After a little more questioning and answering, our meeting was over. Later that day, I got a call from my attorney, who said the agents and prosecutor had contacted him and said they respected my honesty and were going to do everything in their power to help me the best that they could. They realized that I did not have as much involvement as they thought based on their information.

A few more days went by, and my attorney advised me that I needed to hire a pre-sentencing investigator to help me work on my case, and he needed $2,500 to help get this started. When you are charged with a federal crime, the federal court structure uses a pre-sentencing system. Things were getting more profound, and the monies kept flying out of my bank account. "Where would it all end?" I thought to myself. That was the question that kept racing through my head. My heart and spirit were in anguish as this unfolded. Let us pause a few minutes on my tale and turn to your story.

Dear reader, can I grab a cup of coffee with you and let us dialogue for a few minutes? *This one is on me.* Regrets? Do you have any? Come on. Let's keep it real here. Want any do-overs in your narrative? What about a rewind of time? Cher wrote a bestselling song called "If I Could Turn Back Time"? It skyrocketed to the top of the charts. I wonder why? I think it is because we all have deep-seated regrets we wish we could change. I sure did. I think the most challenging part about guilt is that "I should have known better." If something looks too good to be true, then it probably is shady, at best. Like the first time, I made $500 for one hour of activity, pointing people to a birthday party for Fredo. Did that smell like a stinky fish? I think it did!

Nevertheless, at the moment, I went along with it and turned a deaf ear to my inner convictions. It was profoundly foolish. Yes, many of our regrets fall in the foolish bucket. I think that is where the grace of God is the most amazing. Even when I deserve to be punished and corrected, God's love over my life still beats with tenderness and compassion. How do I know that? When my boys acted out, I would advise them out of the same set of ingredients. Empathy and understanding are what God does best.

Here is a bit of Hollywood, Florida news I want to throw into this chapter about my arrest. In the book *Making Jack Falcone*, a New York Times Bestseller, our Hollywood police story is captured in its pages in the chapter called "Going Hollywood" (pages 254 to 275). I am not making this up as you can research or buy the book for yourself. Here is the book's recording of the Hollywood police transactions,

> "*The total bribes paid to the Hollywood police officers fell just below $100,000 for all four men. The actual amounts: Kevin Companion, $42,000; Jeffry Courtney, $22,000; Thomas Simcox, $16,000; Stephen Harrison, $12,000. For these relative pittances, each of the four men faced* **life in prison**.*" (boldness added – page 274)*

When the FBI investigation leak came out, little did I know that my other comrades were making deals with the FBI for lighter sentencing to save their necks, yet I was left in the dark about everything. Here is the actual wording in *Making Jack Falcone*, "*Simcox was already cooperating with us (the FBI), so Companion and Courtney left the fourth member of the enterprise, Stephen Harrison,* **out to dry**.*" (boldness added – page 275)*

Did you catch those two memorable phrases, "life in prison" and "out to dry," in bold print? Those words are found in the likes of a *Lifetime* movie. I have watched many cliffhanger *Lifetime* shows on the ROKU channel, but I was now living my reality movie. From every vantage point, I was in a tight spot, and I knew it. My lawyer would have to work some magic for me on this one if I had any chance of staying out of jail, continuing to provide for my family, and remaining in the police force that I dearly loved. My thirteen years of service to this community were about to be over in a flash of time. I was deeply remorseful.

What was weird for me was remembering how many criminals I had arrested and taken to jail for illegal activity. I looked into their eyes and saw their plight. They were someone's son or daughter. What about a brother or sister? How about a niece or nephew? Could it be a cousin from across town? A next-door neighbor whom you watched grow up. *Criminals come in all shapes and sizes, as I learned on the police force.*

Now, for the first time in my life, I was getting the mug shot. I was the one getting the fingerprints. I was given the criminal numbers to hold up. I was now in the local newspapers. I was the one heading for the federal prison cell. *It was a surreal moment. Was I* arrested? Me? How did I get here? I can hardly believe it. What was next for my life now? What about my wife and my two sons? How would they process all this hurt? At that instant, I was a broken and beaten man. My only hope was a legal miracle, but I did not consider the great plan that God was working over my life.

While I did not like where it was headed, I knew somehow God was still with me and for me. He was working all things out for my good and His Glory. I truly believed that even though the worst was in front of me. Nothing was a surprise to God. I leaned into Him for what lay ahead. As I awaited the forthcoming trial, I tried to keep my sanity and composure for my family's sake, but it was not easy. The pressure on me felt unbearable as I patiently awaited my day in court and my future outcome. Even in this initial stage, God was getting my attention. What was He doing? Was I now on His "blacklist" and in another pile of names? Has Stephen Lynch Harrison Sr. been put in a Heavenly "Time Out"? Oh, how my mind was a whirlwind of reflections and feelings. God help me, please! I sure need YOU.

KEEPING IT REAL!

1. Arrested. Actions do have consequences. Do you have a private life that is dishonoring to God?

2. I was "left out to dry." That sounds harsh! Can God use difficult times for good?

3. Regrets. Do you have any? What can you do today to live without regrets? Name two steps.

4. Can God's love meet you at your deepest need? How do you feel His love now?

5. Satan is a destroyer. Memorize 1 Peter 5:8 (NASB), " [8] Be of sober *spirit*, be on the alert. Your adversary, the devil, prowls around like a roaring lion, *seeking someone to devour.*"

~ Verse to Memorize ~

Keep your heart with all diligence,
For out **of** it *spring* the **issues of life**.
-Proverbs 4:23 (NKJV)

17

FORTY YEARS TO LIFE

For the next six months, my life would never be the same. I lived between two worlds. One world was living as if nothing had ever happened. The other was knowing my trial was scheduled, but it would be six months before it arrived. It is much like your family doctor telling you that cancer has set into your body, and you have six months to live. No, I was not fatal in health, but I can assure you my spirit was dying little by little inside. How do you grapple with such a declaration? The FBI had placed a bounty on my head, and "Life in Prison" was my price tag.

Think about that for a moment. What would you do, and how would you live if you knew that the clock was running out? Time was now my enemy, and the realization that it is now finite wrestled with my soul. How would I live these next six months? Let me give you a stern warning here. I remember reading about a man who had terminal cancer and had a few months to live. In a heartfelt moment with one of his dear friends, the friend asked, "Bobby, what is it like knowing you are dying and that each passing day brings you closer to the end of your life?" In the tenderness of a father to a son, the man riddled with cancer looked up and said, "Tommy, what is it like for you to pretend that you are not living the same way? My life may be shortened, but you are approaching death just as fast as I am." Those sobering words hit

Tommy like a brick. Friend, do not be fooled; you are rapidly moving to your conclusion. These words are chronicled in the book of James 4:13-15 (MSG),

> "¹³⁻¹⁵ And now I have a word for you who brashly announce, 'Today—at the latest, tomorrow—we're off to such and such a city for the year. We're going to start a business and make a lot of money.' You don't know the first thing about tomorrow. *You're nothing but a wisp of fog, catching a brief bit of sun before disappearing.* Instead, make it a habit to say, 'If the Master wills it and we're still alive, we'll do this or that.'"

Do not miss the Scriptures pronouncement here! One translation calls your life a "vapor," a mist that vanishes in milliseconds. You have seen the boiling pot on the stove or old-fashioned tea kettle. The billowing steam dances in the air only to find itself gone before your eyes. It is gone like a flash of lightning on a rainy night. It is gone like the money in your bank account that you earn each month to pay bills. It is gone like the strength that your youth gave you and your gold years pervades you. It is gone like the spouse of fifty-plus years of marriage as death comes calling for its prey. You better ponder the reality of eternity and where you are headed. I share this out of love for you, dear reader.

Once free on bond, I had to make sense of the next six months. First, I needed a job fast to continue to provide for my wife and children. Graciously, my buddy named Donnie offered me employment in his air conditioning company. It was hard work, but I was so grateful to him for the opportunity. He knew of my arrest, but he did not shun me or cast me aside. That is what true friendship is all about. When others see the best and worst of your life and still want to stay engaged, only God can bring that kind of relationship into your life.

Next, I was a wreck, emotionally. I was battling depression, and I needed relief for myself and my family. As you would imagine, my mind was a virtual battleground. I needed some relief, and I needed it now. I had a dear friend named Jay, who knew I was hurting. My wife and I were great friends with him and his wife. Through the years, we became close because Jay was also in law enforcement. Also, we worked out together. It was like a brotherhood. Jay and his wife attended a large church near our home called Calvary Chapel. As members, Jay had come to know Pastor John in a personal way. As I spiraled downward, Jay suggested I speak to Pastor John of Calvary Chapel. I certainly was willing, and Jay called Pastor John to set up the meeting.

Herein lies the problem, Pastor John was unable to meet with me due to some legal proceeding he was involved with. Yet, within three hours, Jay called back and said Pastor John can now meet because the legal dealings had settled out of court. *Only God can intervene in such a manner.* I was overjoyed, and I headed to Calvary Chapel that same night at 6:00 p.m. I was a bit nervous about how everything would shake out if I were frank, but I knew I needed God to give me peace. I was a mess, and it showed.

When I arrived at Calvary Chapel, Pastor John was a beacon of encouragement. He did not condemn me or treat me like an outcast. As I shared the details of my story and my involvement, Pastor John loved me. I felt it. He had a genuine concern for me, my wife, and my two boys. Since our home church had shunned my family and me when all this came out, Pastor John suggested that Calvary Chapel be our arm of support. Boy, did I ever need that ray of hope! From that day, as a family, we attended Calvary Chapel as our home church. It was much needed and a great source of peace for all of us.

It was during our attendance each Sunday at Calvary Chapel that I learned of a unique small group. It met weekly and was specifically for law enforcement families. While not regularly attending such intimate meetings, my wife and I felt the need to join them each week. I can not tell you the love that flowed from that small group of couples toward us. It was like a healing balm that was applied to our souls. My wife and I had never been embraced with such care and concern as this group of people showed us. It was refreshing and stimulating. Each week we met, the bonds of love got stronger and stronger. Dianne and I felt like we belonged to a family who offered us hope during our confusion and time of uncertainty.

I meet with Pastor John every week. *He was like a Spiritual Mentor to me.* Thankfully, he was honest, candid, and transparent. Pastor John shared his checkered past before he gave his life entirely to Jesus Christ. He also said that God gave him the grace to pursue him daily for the next thirty years. It transformed his life, little by little. Pastor John had been at Calvary Chapel for several decades and was instrumental in helping so many people turn their hearts back toward God. I, too, was in that line of grateful individuals.

Pastor John would regularly ask me, "How full is your spiritual cup?" He would say, "Stephen, when your cup is near empty, the devil has greater influence over your life and actions." Boy, was he spot-on! If only I had been in pursuit of God during my times of dealing with Kevin. I believe the Holy Spirit would have given me a stern warning to flee these offers for fast money. However, when you only make God a casual acquaintance, you will end up with everyday wisdom and insight into life's greatest need: TRUTH. Please learn from my mistake here, as it has cost me everything.

With our weekly involvement at Calvary Chapel, our attendance with our law enforcement small group, and my weekly meetings with Pastor John, I can honestly say that God gave me hope and assurance that everything would be alright. No, it did not mean that I was acquitted of my actions. *However, it did mean that God was in control.* I had now relinquished my will into his care along with my wife and children. The months that followed leading up to my trial were not nearly as nerve-racking and emotionally heavy. Nothing had changed outwardly about my situation, *but I can assure you I had begun to change inwardly, and it made all the difference.*

What these six months gave me was time to process and think about my life overall. As mentioned earlier, I did not have a great role model in a father, nor did the insight and instruction growing up prevent such a mishap. Yes, I take full responsibility for my actions, but I pondered what went wrong that left me vulnerable to make such poor choices. I think I learned that I just believed that people would always speak with honesty and integrity. I did not have much exposure to people who would use me or set me up as a puppet to their misdealings as Kevin did. I never had cause to believe he would lie to me. Yet, I was willfully deceived. It was his deception that undermined my life and future. Trickery kills the soul.

For these six months, I could not shake the word: deception, as the Holy Spirit spoke to me. How could I have been so foolish and gullible? Was I naive? Was I easy prey for Kevin and the devil, for that matter? Deception is a nasty word because it destroys individuals and homes every waking moment. It sure had mine as I reflected on my interactions with Kevin. To be deceived is tragic. Dictionary.com calls deception "to mislead by a false appearance or statement; delude." It became crystal clear to me. A false appearance misled me. I was deluded. What does delude mean, "to mislead the mind or judgment of." Kevin had been messing with my mind, delivering half-truths of police details that I genuinely believed were honorable. As I said earlier, *deception kills the soul!* Mine was now bleeding inside.

Let me take a spiritual risk here for a moment. Deception has its origin in Scripture, as found in Genesis. It is a long-standing tactic of your Arch Enemy, Satan. Let us look for a few minutes to learn these truths as Eve, your original Mother, found out the hard way. This conversation is recorded in Genesis 3:1–8 (MSG),

> **3** The serpent was clever, more clever than any wild animal God had made. He spoke to the Woman: "Do I understand that God told you not to eat from any tree in the garden?" [2-3]

The Woman said to the serpent, "Not at all. We can eat from the trees in the garden. It's only about the tree in the middle of the garden that God said, 'Don't eat from it; don't even touch it or you'll die.'" ⁴⁻⁵ The serpent told the Woman, "You won't die. God knows that the moment you eat from that tree, you'll see what's really going on. You'll be just like God, knowing everything, ranging all the way from good to evil." ⁶ When the Woman saw that the tree looked like good eating and realized what she would get out of it—she'd know everything!—she took and ate the fruit and then gave some to her husband, and he ate. ⁷ Immediately the two of them did "see what's really going on"—saw themselves naked! They sewed fig leaves together as makeshift clothes for themselves.

Eve was deceived by the Serpent (Satan). He misled her mind and provided a false appearance of the truth. She believed the lie as fact and acted on it with her entire will. Eve sinned. She also gave it to Adam. He ate of it, too. He sinned. It was a domino effect. The Bible paints this truth about Eve in 1 Timothy 2:13–14 (MSG), "Adam was made first, then Eve; woman was **deceived** first—our pioneer in sin!—with Adam right on her heels." Guess what? Satan still uses good old-fashioned deception today as his primary weapon. As human beings, we still take the bait. In His love, God offers this precaution as noted in Galatians, "⁷ Do not be deceived: God cannot be mocked. A man reaps what he sows. ⁸ Whoever sows to please their flesh, from the flesh will reap destruction; whoever sows to please the Spirit, from the Spirit will reap eternal life" (Galatians 6:7–8 NCV).

As we put the wrap on this chapter, let me give you one other personal observation from these six months. I, Stephen, started this season in the Valley. I was broken. I was beaten. Yet, I was open and available. God was reassuring me that everything was in His hands concerning my future, for my good and His Glory. Why? It had become extremely clear to me that God was working behind the scenes. He was bringing people to us to help us walk through these trying times. Only God can arrange such beautiful outcomes. Yes, I reached a place in God where I was operating in His peace. It felt good, and it felt right. I was mentally preparing for the trial and the road ahead of me. I had accepted that God was with me and God was for me. Conversely, my dear wife, Dianne, had hit a roadblock called Denial. It is the first of the many steps in the grieving process. Real quick. If you are not familiar with the steps of grieving, let me share them. It is from the acronym: D.A.B.D.A.H.

D – Denial
A – Anger
B – Bargaining
D – Depression
A – Acceptance
H – Healing / Hope

Yes, Dianne had started down the roadway of grieving and stalled at the intersection of denial and anger. Tragically, as her husband, I was unable to help her process this level of pain. She knew that her husband, father to her two boys, and the financial provider for all was heading to prison. In her mind, the "Life in Prison" edict was haunting her from every side. In her defense, no woman should ever have to ponder such a heavy load. It is mind-numbing. Inwardly, my sweet wife had died a thousand deaths. The only glimmer of hope was our church involvement and small group meetings. Thankfully, they never left Dianne alone in her processing of this tragedy. The ladies surrounded her with care, hope, and affirmation.

One final thought about these pivotal six months. It struck me that our God has a right hand and a left hand. He is not limited in His ability to make all things work together for His Glory. Remember,

God has a Right Hand of Favor and a Left Hand of Action. He considers everything and brings about an expected end. Here are two verses to end with that I clung to as I awaited my trial. They are as follows in Jeremiah 29:11 (NIV) and Romans 8:28 (NIV),

> "[11] 'For I know the plans I have for you,' declares the LORD, 'plans to prosper you and not to harm you, plans to give you hope and a future.'"

> "[28] And we know that in all things, God works for the good of those who love him, who have been called according to his purpose."

Let us move on to the Trial of My Life!

KEEPING IT REAL!

1. How full is your spiritual cup? Could you have been deceived too?

2. Pastor John became my spiritual mentor. Would you be open to having one? Why or why not?

3. Deception! What comes to your mind when you think of this word? How would you strive to prevent this in your life?

4. Sowing and Reaping. Do you get back what is sown? What kinds of seeds are you planting now?

5. Denial. Do you live in denial in any area of your life? What should you do about it? What advice would you have given Dianne?

~ Verse to Memorize ~

[14] Do not enter the path of the wicked, And do not walk in the way of evil. [15] Avoid it, do not travel on it; Turn away from it and pass on. -Proverbs 4:14–15 (NKJV)

18

MY TRIAL OF THE CENTURY

My day of reckoning had finally come. All the thoughts that swirled in my head these past six months would culminate on July 21, 2007. The time was 9:00 a.m. I would say that I was ready for this day to be over. In my mind, I played out a dozen different scenarios, from only getting prolonged probation to spending a lifetime behind bars. Let me share a few story details leading up to my trial, and then I will give you a full disclosure of my day in the courtroom.

The final caveat of my six-month waiting period was my need for surgery on my shoulder. From my prior years of weightlifting, coupled with the demands of my job working to install air condition units, I was in dire pain, and I needed relief. The US Attorney had advised me to go ahead and get the surgery taken care of before the trial. As push came to shove, I could get it scheduled, but the surgery date would fall on July 20, 2007. Yes, if you calculated that right in your mind, it was the day before my trial. Looking back, that was probably not the best outcome, but I knew it was necessary for my overall health. To compound matters a bit, I was given pain medicine to take as needed, but I was reluctant to take anything the morning of the trial to be fully engaged and mentally alert for that day. Nevertheless, I was in extreme pain throughout the trial.

The fateful morning had finally arrived, and I must confess that the night before was wrought with sleeplessness. Put yourself in my shoes! You would be hard-pressed to find any sleep, too. Even with the prayer support, personal encouragement, and well-wishes, I knew I was heading to the moment of all moments in my life. Forty years to life was not just the catchy title of Chapter 17. It was what I was facing this day.

Having dressed up for this momentous occasion, Dianne and I arrived at the courthouse. We had prearranged to meet outside in the parking lot with a small band of friends, church members, Pastor John, and Connie, his wife. This time was bathed with prayer and seeking God for His guidance. I reassured the group that I put the outcome in God's hands and that I would embrace it with God's provision, whatever happens. I know that sounds like a cliché, but I was sincere in my declaration.

As we entered the courtroom, there was a standing-room-only crowd already in place. This trial was BIG news in Hollywood, Florida, and the media people were in full swing to cover the story in extensive detail. For someone who had never been in trouble with the law, it was overwhelming. It was a feeding frenzy as the chatter from the audience entered my ears. The small talk all around me seemed so hollow as we awaited the arrival of the judge. Kevin Companion and his attorney, along with his wife Emily, were on my left. I was seated next to my attorney, Ed O'Donnell. My wife, Dianne, would be right behind me.

It would be of interest to note that Kevin Companion was considered to be the ring leader, according to the FBI, of this police corruption story. Why is that so significant? Generally, a person is tried before a judge, one-on-one. Yet, on this day, to expedite the outcome, they combined Kevin and me in the same courtroom setting. I always thought that to be strange and wondered if that impacted the judge's judgment concerning my involvement. *The trial began as the judge entered the courtroom.*

The next three hours seemed like an eternity. Kevin would go first in this lengthy debate. Person after person would give testimony in defense of Kevin's character, community involvement, church affiliation, and family influence. Kevin was a "good" person who got fascinated with a fast life and fast money. This kind of living always has a payout. When the dust settled, the judge pronounced over Kevin a 168-month sentence. Do the math. *That is fourteen years in confinement.* The courtroom gasped, and the silence was defining. My heart broke for Kevin, his wife, and his children. Their lives would never be the same again. *It also made me wonder about my chances.*

Finally, the judge looked in my direction. His eyes pierced through my soul, and it was paralyzing. I cannot describe to you the feeling at that moment. My mind did a quick mental flashback, from early childhood to the present day. How did I arrive at this setting? Me? A police officer, of all things!

What could have been different in my early childhood that might have prevented such a tragedy like today? Had my father been sober and engaged in my upbringing, would I have turned out another way? Could I have then seen through Kevin's lies and deception? If I had taken my church involvement with more sincerity and interest, could God have played a more significant role in my life up until now? Did I see confession as a big waste of time rather than a warning that sinful behavior has its ultimate consequences in life? Sin indeed does lead to death.

I also considered the past thirteen years of community service as a decorated police officer. I loved my job, and I loved the people I served in Hollywood, Florida. It was more than a career for me, and I invested my all into its outcome. I keep our community safe and free from gangs and criminal activity, drug trafficking, and street violence. Additionally, I had met some wonderful people whom I worked alongside. They were not just my peers, but also my friends. We hung out and did life together. It was fulfilling and plentiful with memories.

I cherished every moment of its journey. I had no regrets about my occupation choice.

Finally, I pondered the effects this moment would have on my marriage to Dianne and my two sons' health and well-being, still being very young and impressionable. Who would now provide for their needs? Who would be there to bring them protection and comfort? What would their future look like if I am sentenced to time behind bars? *My heart was about to explode in my chest as I grappled with such misery, loneliness, and shame.* The courtroom was filled with people I loved, and this was NOT how I envisioned my adult life unfolding. No, this day was a harsh reminder that SIN KILLS. It takes no prisoners. It longs for your life to take it and rejoice over your disgraceful exposure. I felt it all in a flash as the judge called my name: Stephen L. Harrison Sr.

My attorney, Ed O'Donnell, took the lead and invited character witnesses to speak on my behalf. One by one, they assured the judge that "Stephen Lynch Harrison Sr." was remorseful and apologetic over his actions and behavior in this alleged activity. They spoke of my newly found walk with God and my six-month mentorship with Pastor John of Calvary Chapel. Others commented on our family involvement in Calvary Chapel, small group meetings, and volunteering in the community as Calvary Chapel served its citizens of Hollywood, Florida. It was moving and emotional. I had made many friends.

Even my dad, at the moment, battling stage four cancer, addressed the judge on my behalf. The judge, gracious in his tone towards my dad, sincerely thanked him for taking the time to stand with his son in this horrific ordeal. Their words were compelling and gripping as these two men spoke as "father-to-father" and left the legal jargon behind for a brief instant. Time stood still as their words filled the air. Tears flowed from those in the courtroom as their sentiments touched the depths of each soul. In confession, I lost it myself. No father dreams of such an occurrence. You cannot prepare for such a time as this. There are no dress rehearsals that can be scripted for dads over their son's challenging plight before a judge. However, it was happening before my watching eyes. It broke me deeply inside.

As the witnesses finalized their assertions, it was now my time to stand and speak. Rising to my feet, I looked at the judge and began, "Your Honor, I stand before you today accepting full responsibility for my actions as charged in these proceedings. It would be my desire that you consider the testimonies from my friends and family. I ask you for leniency and mercy over the sentencing." Next, I said, "Your Honor, I have thirteen years of police participation and service to the community of Hollywood, Florida. I have earned medals of accommodation and merit. I am a decorated police veteran who acted with poor judgment, trusting a person who was now deemed to be untrustworthy. I thanked the judge for listening to my sentiments today."

What happened next was unprecedented. The US attorney who was prosecuting my case and the two FBI agents stood up and asked the judge if they could speak to the court on my behalf. The judge said that he didn't need to hear more about Stephen and that the court had rendered a sentence.

The judge had me stand for the sentencing. He began, "I find Stephen Lynch Harrison Sr. guilty of criminal activity and with this, I sentence him to serve one hundred and eight months in federal prison." For those wondering, that is the equivalent of nine years in custody. My shock was evident as the courtroom sighed in disbelief. My attorney mumbled words in dismay as well. *This judgment was not supposed to happen.* What about all the character witnesses and my father's conversation with the judge? What about my testimony about accepting responsibility for my actions? Did any of that matter to the judge? I can only surmise, "Apparently not!" *What a travesty that was unfolding. I was now headed to federal prison. I was speechless.*

I was asked to take off my sports coat. My shoulder was still in a sling. Next, I was told to take off all my jewelry and give it to Dianne behind me. The deputies approached me and placed the cuffs on my hands and feet. I was escorted out of the courtroom as my wife, the gang of friends, supporters, and Pastor John and Connie watched in disbelief. This present storyline was not how it was supposed to end. God, "Help me." I was not prepared for this outcome. What now? What next? How can I make it?" Not all stories end with "Happily Ever After." I would now spend my next three thousand two hundred and eighty-five days behind bars. *In a few words, "I was humbled and numb."*

Dear reader, let us take a few brief minutes and talk about the hardships and difficulties that come your way. Is God on the hook to make your wishes come exactly as you desire? Is He more like the *I Dream of Jeannie* show where you keep getting your wishes at the hands of a personal assistant or "Jeannie"? That would be nice! Well, maybe if you live in Hollywood, California. However, in Hollywood, Florida, that was not how the magic was working. I was now headed to prison, and God was still in control, despite what it looked like at this very moment. In the book of Job, the author shares a controversial question,

> "⁹ Then his wife said to him, 'Do you still hold fast to your integrity? Curse God and die!' ¹⁰ But he said to her, 'You speak as one of the foolish women speaks. **Shall we indeed accept good from God, and shall we not accept adversity?'** *In all this, Job did not sin with his lips*" (Job 2:9–10 NKJV).

Let me restate that emboldened line in my own words, "Life should only be about having good fortune, and everything negative is not welcome, God." How is that for a prayer to the Creator of the Universe? You may think, "God, you owe me only good things." Yes, that is what we expect from our Heavenly Fathers. If we were brutally honest, that is our mindset and heart posture. We want God to be our Heavenly filter, only permitting pleasant things to fall into our lives and "filter" out the negative stuff. I may be meddling here a bit, but you know what I am saying is true. We all think this way about God. If God is "good," then why does terrible stuff have to enter our proverbial picture of the good life? Ouch, that may have stung a little. So, let me give you a word picture to wrestle down. *In your relationship with God, do you have a Heavenly Father or a Heavenly Filter?*

Friend, I can so relate to you at this juncture. Think back to my trial and its outcome. If I were candid about that day, I wanted God to be my Heavenly Filter, more than my Heavenly Father. Can you see the difference? A birth father takes a more extended look at his child's needs and offers the best results for long-term outcomes. No, they are not always seen as enjoyable or warm and fuzzy at the twinkling you face. They never are!

Nonetheless, the bigger picture shows the necessary ingredients from God's viewpoint. He sees your end from your beginning. Why? That is because everything about your life is past tense to God. He knew you before the foundations of the world were framed. You were not a random consideration because your parents were intimate. No, no, no. God is unpacking your life according to His divine image and storyline. The canvas of your life is emerging with each brushstroke of bright colors along with the darker shades that offer contrast. They ALL are needed to create the majestic outcome.

In the book of James, Jesus's half-brother penned these powerful words in James 1:2–3 (MSG),

> "Consider it a sheer gift, friends, when tests and challenges come at you from all sides. You know that under pressure, your faith-life is forced into the open and shows its true colors. So don't try to get out of anything prematurely. Let it do its work, so you become mature and well-developed, not deficient in any way."

Mature? Well-developed? Forced into the open space? What kind of spiritual walk with God do you want? Take just a few minutes and ponder that question. Is He your Heavenly Father or your Heavenly Filter? Is He personal or just functional? Do you want Him close by or casually near, only when needed? Do you want your faith to be anorexic or anemic? Do you long for a weak faith or one full with power by the demonstrations of the Holy Spirit in your life, chiseling away the junk and the funk that tarnishes your vessel's usefulness? True faith in God results from a surrendered life, holding nothing back, and taking NO substitute routes to maximize your God-given potential. Let me list the above verses one more time in James 1:2–4. This time, let us use another translation as recorded in the New King James Version,

"² My brethren, **count it all joy** when you fall into various trials, ³ knowing that the testing of your faith produces patience. ⁴ But let patience have *its* perfect work, that you may be perfect and complete, *lacking nothing*."

And as written in 1 Corinthians 4:7–17 (NKJV),

"⁷ But we have this treasure in earthen vessels, that the excellence of the power may be of God and not of us. ⁸ *We are* hard-pressed on every side, yet not crushed; *we are* perplexed, but not in despair; ⁹ persecuted, but not forsaken; struck down, but not destroyed— ¹⁰ always carrying about in the body the dying of the Lord Jesus, that the life of Jesus also may be manifested in our body. ¹¹ For we who live are always delivered to death for Jesus's sake, that the life of Jesus also may be manifested in our mortal flesh. ¹² So then death is working in us, but life in you.

"¹³ And since we have the same spirit of faith, according to what is written, 'I believed and therefore I spoke,' we also believe and therefore speak, ¹⁴ knowing that He who raised up the Lord Jesus will also raise us up with Jesus, and will present *us* with you. ¹⁵ For all things *are* for your sakes, that grace, having spread through the many, may cause thanksgiving to abound to the glory of God.

"ⁱ⁶ Therefore, we do not lose heart. Even though our outward man is perishing, yet the inward *man* is being renewed day by day. ¹⁷ For our light affliction, which is but for a moment, is working for us a far more exceeding *and* eternal weight of glory, ¹⁸ while we do not look at the things which are seen, but at the things which are not seen. For the things which are seen *are* temporary, but the things which are not seen *are* eternal."

God is working in you a far greater weight of glory, His Glory, and Your good. Do not shun His loving hand of correction as it holds in its power the fruit of righteousness, internal peace, and eternal hope. These three will not disappoint you when each has grown into its fullest expression. Righteousness, peace, and hope are in short supply these days, but with God on your side, He is working it out in the due season. Lean into His care over your life.

Little did I know, at the time, that God had gone before me and had begun to orchestrate my "comeback" story. Yes, He did, but I was unaware of a God who cared so much for His creation, down to every single person on Planet Earth. The Lord was putting people and places together to minister to me while in my prison days. Do not miss that detail. Even when you have made a poor decision or totally messed something up, God is working behind the scenes to create a stellar outcome on your behalf. It reminds me of the bridge in the song, "Way Maker" which states:

> Even when I don't see it, You're workin'
> Even when I don't feel it, You're workin'
> You never stop, You never stop workin'
> You never stop.
> Even when I don't see it, You're workin'

Even when I don't feel it, You're workin'
You never stop, You never stop workin'
You never stop,

Then the chorus of that song declares a fantastic truth about your life, all the time and every time. God is not limited when you are at your darkest hour or in a tight spot, even if you are heading to prison for the next nine years, as I was. This truth always prevails:

Jesus, You are…
Way Maker, Miracle Worker
Promise Keeper, Light in the Darkness
My God, that is who You are
(I know, I know You are)
Way Maker, Miracle Worker
Promise Keeper, Light in the Darkness
My God, that is who You are
Yeah, that is who You are
Jesus that is who You are

As we wind down this chapter, let me end with this truth. *Not all prisons have four walls.* My guest writer, Bud, shares a story about when he was getting his Master of Arts in Marriage and Family Counseling. While having to take a course in group counseling as part of his assignments, Bud attended a support group of his choosing. He was to go to four different meetings throughout a month-long period. Bud shared that his brother, Mark, had struggled with alcohol for over three decades and finally got help at Alcoholics Anonymous (AA). Bud went to four AA meetings to better understand his brother's plight and battle to be free from alcohol. Each session was eye-opening and awe inspiring. Each person was raw, frank, and to the point. It is what I like to say, "Keeping It Real." In any event, one person made the statement, "Not all prisons have four walls. Many in prisons are freer than those walking around in independence on the outside. Why? Because persons on the outsides of those four walls are prisoners to their addictions, minds, and behaviors."

As Bud was sitting beside this courageous gentleman that day, he was touched to the core of his soul. "Not all prisons have four walls" would never leave his thinking. Dear reader, what about you? You may not be heading to prison as I was that day. However, that does not mean you are not a "prisoner" of some kind. Your freedom may have been taken away by your thought life or what I like to call "Mental Incarceration." One negative thought after another, sabotaging your present and destroying your future.

Additionally, your liberty may have been given over to alcohol, as Bud's new friend would admit. Maybe even the prescription drugs that once cured physical pain are now trying to curb mental and emotional distress. Yes, if you were to take a few minutes of honest inventory, you would be able to describe your "prison" in full detail. This activity would be a sobering one because you know it exists, but you have never taken the time to identify its impact on your life, family, and outlook. Yes, "Not all prisons have four walls!" However, as I will learn while in prison, Jesus Christ is the Chain Breaker. That leads me to the song of the same title. Let these words sink into your spirit as a human being. Read below verses 1 and 2.

Chain Breaker
Song by Zach Williams

Verse # 1

If you've been walking the same old road for miles and miles
If you've been hearing the same old voice tell the same old lies

If you're trying to fill the same old holes inside
There's a better life
There's a better life

Verse # 2

We've all searched for the light of day in the dead of night
We've all found ourselves worn out from the same old fight
We've all run to things we know just ain't right
And there's a better life
There's a better life

Friend, I am convinced you are shaking your head in agreement here. You have been there. I have been there. I can honestly say as I was heading to prison that I echoed the words of this song. It rang so true in my personal life. So, precious friend, then what is the remedy to life's plight? It can be found in the chorus of this powerful song.

Chorus

If you've got pain
He's a pain taker
If you feel lost
He's a way maker
If you need freedom or saving
He's a prison-shaking Savior
If you've got chains
He's a chain breaker

Yes, Jesus Christ is the pain taker, way maker, and chain breaker. Inviting Him into your heart and life is the best thing you will ever do.

If your heart is pounding out of your chest right now and your spirit is tender toward God's offer for a better life, then I would encourage you to stop right now and turn to the end of the book to Chapter 26, "Meeting Jesus Christ," and read how to have a personal relationship with God, through His Son, Jesus Christ. Get that relationship settled, this very instant, over your life. You will NEVER regret your commitment to follow Jesus Christ with your life and entrust your future to His care, love, and instruction.

Now, let us move on to my life in jail.

KEEPING IT REAL!

1. Trials. They come in many shapes and sizes. Why does God use trials to change us?

2. Fear paralyzes. How would you have dealt with the fear if you were in my shoes?

3. I said, "I had 'peace' no matter the outcome." Could you have been so calm?

4. "Count it all joy"? For real? Is God asking too much? Why can we be joyful during hard times?

5. How clean is your Vessel? Could it be that God is purifying your life with tests? Why or why not?

~ Verse to Memorize ~

[18] But the path of the just *is* like the shining sun, That shines ever brighter unto the perfect day. [19] The way of the wicked *is* like darkness; They do not know what makes them stumble.
-Proverbs 4: 18–19 (NKJV)

19

GOING TO PRISON

When the dust settled from the trial and my mind was catching up to what had just happened, I needed to make peace with the fact that I was going to spend several years behind bars. I cannot put into words what was running through my head as I was told I was headed to the Federal Bureau of Prison's Miami Detention Center. I would be staying on the eleventh floor initially where all the high-profile cases were housed. This was also for my own security. As you know, convicts don't take too kindly to police officers who are now behind bars with them. In fact, I just knew that my life was in danger if not properly secured.

I certainly did not know how long I would be housed here until a formal prison location was determined for me. Yet, no matter where you start, prison life can be a hard living on the mind and human spirit. You just don't get mentally and emotionally prepared for what it is going to be like. We were created for freedom and mobility, to embrace life to the fullest and make memories that touch the soul. It is what God envisioned for our lives as human beings. Freedom of any kind is priceless. I never would have believed I would find myself in this predicament. Me? Of all people!

And, to make matters more challenging, I was placed in the same holding cell with Kevin Companion for my first fourteen days. Can you see me, now, lodging with Kevin as my new "prison" roommate? Remember Kevin, the ring leader of the Hollywood police scandal. The same Kevin at my trial who got sentenced to one hundred and sixty-eight months of prison time. The one and only Kevin who had repeatedly lied to me about the shady off-duty assignments. Yes, Kevin was the last person I wanted to see in my life anymore. Yet, something odd began to happen inside of me. I began to have compassion for Kevin as he was a shattered and defeated man. At least, during my imprisonment, I had a personal relationship with Jesus Christ. Kevin had nothing to draw from for strength and hope. He was alone.

I found myself beginning to pray for Kevin and sharing the love of Jesus Christ with him. Kevin was scared, and he was receptive to my sharing. From this position of surrender to God, I could overlook what he did to me and see his more significant need for salvation and peace. I planted some eternal seeds over him for the two weeks we were together. He needed God's forgiveness and hope moving forward. As a result of our close contact, I was a representative of Jesus Christ in a profound way. Eventually, Kevin and I would move to differing floors, but I believed that God put us together for that small period to make peace with each other. You never know what God is going to ask you to do, even if you have been wronged. It reminds me of the Scripture as noted in Matthew 5:43–48 (NIV),

> "[43] You have heard that it was said, 'Love your neighbor and hate your enemy.' [44] But I tell you, love your enemies and pray for those who persecute you, [45] that you may be children of your Father in heaven. He causes his sun to rise on the evil and the good, and sends rain on the righteous and the unrighteous. [46] If you love those who love you, what reward will you get? Are not even the tax collectors doing that? [47] And if you greet only your own people, what are you doing more than others?

Do not even pagans do that? **⁴⁸** Be perfect, therefore, as your heavenly Father is perfect."

Love your enemies! Can you do that? Are you willing to do it? That is why those who make fun of Christianity as a weak-minded faith and for those who need a spiritual crutch in life have never studied the harder saying of Scripture. It takes a new nature to do what goes against human nature. I was born from above. I was in Christ and He was in me. I have His nature in my heart and soul. Friend, as I was seeking God for myself, I could not help but love Kevin into wholeness and completeness in Christ, too. No, I don't know for 100 percent certain that Kevin surrendered his life to Christ over that two-week time, but I clearly shared what was needed to have that kind of life. The rest would be up to God.

Do you know what else God was doing during that two-week period? He was giving me a chance to exercise His word over my life. What words you may wonder? Seventy Times Seven. They will be listed below for your viewing as recorded in Matthew 18:21–35 (NKJV),

"**²¹** Then Peter came to Him and said, 'Lord, how often shall my brother sin against me, and I forgive him? Up to seven times?' **²²** Jesus said to him, 'I do not say to you, up to seven times, **but up to seventy times seven.**' **²³** Therefore the kingdom of heaven is like a certain king who wanted to settle accounts with his servants. **²⁴** And when he had begun to settle accounts, one was brought to him who owed him ten thousand talents. **²⁵** But as he was not able to pay, his master commanded that he be sold, with his wife and children and all that he had, and that payment be made. **²⁶** The servant therefore fell down before him, saying, 'Master, have patience with me, and I will pay you all.' **²⁷** Then the master of that servant was moved with compassion, released him, and forgave him the debt.

[28] "But that servant went out and found one of his fellow servants who owed him a hundred denarii; and he laid hands on him and took *him* by the throat, saying, 'Pay me what you owe!' [29] So his fellow servant fell down at his feet and begged him, saying, 'Have patience with me, and I will pay you all.' [30] And he would not, but went and threw him into prison till he should pay the debt. [31] So when his fellow servants saw what had been done, they were very grieved, and came and told their master all that had been done. [32] Then his master, after he had called him, said to him, 'You wicked servant! I forgave you all that debt because you begged me. [33] Should you not also have had compassion on your fellow servant, just as I had pity on you?' [34] And his master was angry, and delivered him to the torturers until he should pay all that was due to him. [35] 'So My heavenly Father also will do to you if each of you, from his heart, does not forgive his brother his trespasses.'"

Four hundred and ninety times is a lot to forgive someone! Is that what Jesus was asking of me toward Kevin Companion now? No! That number is elevated, but not nearly enough. How do I know that? In the Bible story above, the first gentleman owed a debt to the king that he was unable to pay in his entire lifetime of working his job. In other words, it was insurmountable to be eliminated. That means he was now stuck in a bad place. His debt was unforgivable, unless the king, in his compassion, was willing to write off the debt in full. Guess what? He was and he did. He took the debt completely to zero out of love and mercy. The servant was forgiven of the entire amount. What a merciful king! What a gracious king. What a picture of our loving Heavenly Father toward us. Forgive as you have been forgiven is the mandate here. No wiggle room. No work-arounds. As God has forgiven you, then go and do likewise.

Every night as I lay my head on my pillow, God was asking me to forgive Kevin of his misdealings with me. He not only needed God's forgiveness, he also needed mine, too. Would I be like the servant who was begging the king (God) for forgiveness of a debt he could never repay, and then turn around and demand of the one who owed mere pennies to pay in full? WOW! That is not an easy pill to swallow, but it is a fair comparison, nonetheless. Yes, God wanted me to let Kevin loose and walk in freedom with me. I needed to forgive Kevin, the man who helped land me behind bars to begin with.

I think it is safe to say that forgiveness is an intellectual decision followed by an emotional process. Yes, I can say I forgive Kevin and I did, but let me also say that it took time for the emotions of the situation to go away. That was not an overnight process, not in the least. It would take some time for the internal battle to subside about my life now that I am serving time for crimes I had been deceived to do. Nevertheless, I would model the way of Jesus Christ and love as He loved me.

It would be almost right at five months for me to get conformation of my prison location. I thought a lot about my two weeks with Kevin and what lay ahead for both of us. I am grateful that I had the Lord on my side and that He would be my comfort and strength. Let's move on to My New Life Behind Bars.

KEEPING IT REAL!

1. Roommates with Kevin. Could you have done that? How would you have responded to him during that two-week period?
2. Love your enemies. Is the Word of God being unrealistic in its claim? Why or why not?
3. I said that I began to feel compassion for Kevin and began to pray for him. What about you?
4. Can you relate to the story of the king and the servant? Do you want something you are not giving?
5. Forgiveness is a BIG topic in my life. How do you process forgiveness in your own world?

~ *Verse to Memorize* ~

Blessed *is he whose* transgression *is* **forgive**n, *Whose* sin *is* covered.
-Psalms 32:1 (NKJV)

20

MY NEW LIFE BEHIND BARS

I cannot put into words what was running through my head as I headed to the United States Penitentiary (USP) in Atlanta, Georgia. We boarded a large aircraft that had all the windows completely blacked out. It was like an aero-hearse, and the men who were boarding the plane were heading to their "funeral." The inside of the plane had no seats. We were cuffed to the walls of this flying bird and sat on the floor. As I left Miami, I was heavy with grief and fear as my new life was emerging, at least for the next several years. I knew that while heading toward Atlanta, my life would forever be changed.

The USP in Atlanta was a shocking place to start my incarceration. It was nicknamed the "Atlanta Holdover" Facility. Any prisoner, regardless of his destination, must make his way through Atlanta initially. My friend, this was no five-star hotel. It was not even a half-star hotel. No, if you were to look around, you would have been stunned. You have to remember that I was never in trouble with the law, even as a teenager. Additionally, in law enforcement, I never saw this side of the prison system. I did not know what to expect if I were completely honest.

The Atlanta Holdover Facility was 100 percent nasty, despicable, inhumane, and just plain disgusting. Words do not describe this place accurately. It was so overcrowded that I got stuffed in a cell with a total of four men. With only two cell bunks, guess who was sleeping on the floor for the next two weeks? As the cell had a limited footprint for space, I found myself sleeping on a concrete floor next to the toilet. There were large holes in the walls where rats would make their way into the cell, but the use of old milk cartons would serve the trick of blocking the gaps. Also, the cockroaches were hosting nightly meetings in my cell as I lay on the floor. I put tissue paper in my ears to block the noise.

To make matters worse, if one of the "cellies" (prison slang for a cellmate) needed to use the toilet, you lay there and held your nose until the aroma passed. This duration was going to be a long two weeks for me. I had to shoulder this, though. The time spent in this confined space was quite challenging for me. If you do not like cramped spaces, sharing a cell with three other men would create much anxiety. It sure did for me. In this transitory state, the cellies rarely talked to one another. So, you feel alone, isolated, ashamed, and remorseful. Most cellies sleep the entire time except for the one hour given for recreation each day, defined to an enclosed area.

Consequently, showers were only permitted twice per week for five minutes. The darkness of this initial moment was looming over me. "If this is the beginning, what is the rest of the journey going to be like?" I wondered! I was a detailed and clean individual. I bathed often, and now I would have reduced clothing and bathing opportunities. The body odor of my new cellmates filled our cell. I would somehow have to manage these unique and trying circumstances. Yet, I knew God was with me.

It was in this context that God reminded me of Psalms 139: 1–18 (NIV),

> "[1] You have searched me, Lord,
> and you know me.
> [2] You know when I sit and when I rise;

you perceive my thoughts from afar.
³ You discern my going out and my lying down;
you are familiar with all my ways.
⁴ Before a word is on my tongue
you, LORD, know it completely.
⁵ You hem me in behind and before,
and you lay your hand upon me.
⁶ Such knowledge is too wonderful for me,
too lofty for me to attain.
⁷ *Where can I go from your Spirit?*
Where can I flee from your presence?
⁸ If I go up to the heavens, you are there;
if I make my bed in the depths, you are there.
⁹ If I rise on the wings of the dawn,
if I settle on the far side of the sea,
¹⁰ even there your hand will guide me,
your right hand will hold me fast.
¹¹ If I say, 'Surely the darkness will hide me
and the light becomes night around me,'
¹² even the darkness will not be dark to you;
the night will shine like the day,
for darkness is as light to you.
¹³ *For you created my inmost being;*
you knit me together in my mother's womb.
¹⁴ *I praise you because I am fearfully and wonderfully made;*
your works are wonderful,
I know that full well.
¹⁵ My frame was not hidden from you
when I was made in the secret place,
when I was woven together in the depths of the earth.
¹⁶ Your eyes saw my unformed body;
all the days ordained for me were written in your book

before one of them came to be.
¹⁷ How precious to me are your thoughts, God!
How vast is the sum of them!
¹⁸ Were I to count them,
they would outnumber the grains of sand—
when I awake, **I am still with you.**"

Those last five words became my shelter and my therapy, "I am still with you." Even in my darkest hour, as I began my one hundred and eight months as a convict in the federal prison system, *I knew that God was still with me.* It became the air I breathed each day. This thought was echoed in Psalms 46:1–3, "¹ God is our refuge and strength, an ever-present help in trouble. ² Therefore we will not fear, though the earth give way and the mountains fall into the heart of the sea, ³ though its waters roar and foam and the mountains quake with their surging." I drank in God's word like never before in my life. It brought me peace.

Let me introduce you to a term in the prison system. It is called *Diesel therapy.* Have you ever heard of it? It would not come up in most social settings, but it is part of the language in prison life. To quote Mark Whitaker in his book, *Mark Whitaker: Against All Odds,* "Diesel therapy is the cruelest aspect of being a federal inmate. Diesel therapy is a nightmare involving shackles, deprivation, and weeks or months of getting bused and flown through a zigzag maze of interim moves and holdover jails. Diesel therapy has no directional logic. It is pure punishment, and the guards made sure you get demeaned at every step of the process." I got my hands on a copy of Mark's book while behind bars, and his prison story captivated me. I, too, would have my share of Diesel therapy over the next seven years of my life.

My first bout with Diesel therapy would land me in the federal prison in Williamsburg, South Carolina. Being from Hollywood, Florida, any prison assignment's goal is to be less than five hundred miles from your family. If you have any hope of trying to keep your family intact and together, there must be opportunities for personal visits and recreational activity when able. My first prison assignment put me almost 630 miles away from my wife, Dianne, and my two boys. That distance alone would make it challenging to maintain some level of marital and family life. It concerned me greatly as I entered this initial period of penitentiary life. My tenure at Williamsburg, South Carolina, lasted until September 2009. From there, I was able to chisel away thirty-one months of my one hundred and eight months sentence.

Some life-challenging things happened during this season at Williamsburg, South Carolina. As mentioned during the trial, my father was in stage four cancer, and his ability to defend this debilitating disease culminated in March 2009. I was now faced with the harrowing predicament of attending the funeral and saying farewell to my father. Inmates do not get time off for funerals if they have been incarcerated for less than twenty-four months.

Nevertheless, God stepped up in a BIG way. I still put in for the request to attend my dad's funeral. The prison officials in Williamsburg denied my initial request. Yet, my prior judge got wind of my father dying and granted me leave for several days to visit my family and attend the funeral. I was given a pass to travel for several days and ultimately return when my time was up. *That is unheard of for inmates who have just started to serve their time behind bars. Nevertheless, God showed me favor with the judge, and I got to say goodbye to my dad. I am so thankful for that.*

As I enjoyed my time of leave, I sensed something was different with my wife, Dianne. She seemed distant and disconnected from me. Yes, I had been away for a while. However, we always tried to stay connected over the phone and through writing. In the book *Mark Whitaker: Against All Odds*, his wife and children supported him faithfully for nine years, often moving near his next Diesal therapy exercise. Her devotion to him was unprecedented. Prison statistics show that spouses usually disengage from married life within thirty-six months of incarceration and then file for divorce. I was working hard to prevent such an occurrence with Dianne, but her behavior was concerning me during this leave. In any event, the time was enjoyable, visiting with old friends and family members. As it marched to a close, I kissed my wife and boys. Then, I boarded the bus to make my way back to Williamsburg, South Carolina.

With hours of riding ahead of me, my mind had time to process the past several days. Now my father went to be with the Lord, and my mother has to fend for herself. After fifty years of marriage, this would not be easy for her to bear. This thought brought additional stress into my world. I truly loved my mother. Not to mention, Dianne was up to something, and I knew it. Was she preparing to exit the marriage like many of the spouses do with inmates? Did our fifteen years of marriage mean anything to her along with our bearing of children together? What would the boys think? We were soul mates, or so I thought. I would learn the hard way that I was standing alone when I went to prison. Yes, they cared. However, I would have to shoulder the aloneness, emotional despair, and passage of time. Visits from loved ones were infrequent or almost non-existent in my world. Prison life has a way of "raping" the human soul if I were candid. Like so many places in the Scriptures, I had to cling to, "But God." It was my only hope, my source of peace, and my daily bread. But God had my back as I headed back to Williamsburg.

I settled back into the grind of life behind bars. I was the encourager to those inmates who were trying to cope just like I was. Yet, God was my sustenance as I drank from the Well of Scripture. From that, I was able to give away His goodness to others. I felt a purpose behind the words of life I could offer. I was actively involved in our church services on Sunday and engaged in the choir as opportunities arose. I made every attempt to immerse my mind, soul, and spirit in the things of God. It kept my mind focused on healthy topics. If not for

God, my world would have imploded. Nevertheless, I was not without challenges. Yet, I knew they could all be conquered with God.

My suspicion was correct with Dianne. She had gotten involved with a friend of mine, and they were now a couple. To my dismay, I was served with divorce papers from my "Best Friend" and the mother of my children. I could not believe it because we had been through so much together. I stared at those papers for hours. Yes, her signature was on the documents. She wanted out. I had the proof in front of me.

During one of our final dialogues, I said something to the effect of "I will not be able to see the boys any longer." Over the next several days that passed, I was being watched more tightly. Then came the call from the warden's office. Stephen, "We have the recorded conversation of you saying, 'I will not be able to see the boys any longer.' We are concerned that you are suicidal and are putting you in solitary confinement for observation."

I was furious with the warden. I was not going to harm myself. I explained to them that my words were taken out of context. I was going through a divorce, and my wife was taking my boys from me. That was obvious. However, when the dust settled, they would not hear me out. I was put into the "Hole," as we call it in prison terms. My heart was fractured, but I knew God could make beauty from these ashes. I leaned into Him during the time in solitary confinement. Lord, I need you. This life is hard!

The warden labeled me a "troublemaker" and a potential problem to their jail location from this unfortunate incident. As time would eventually tell, I was about to experience another "Deisel therapy." You guessed it. I was headed back to the Atlanta Holding Facility for two weeks, en route to my next home. As it turned out, the Atlanta Holding Facility had not gotten any nicer. Yes, all the same conditions applied for my two weeks of stay. I just closed my "eyes" and "grit" my teeth. It is one of those things where you find the courage and endure it. It was there that I learned I was heading to North Carolina. It was a prison for the mentally ill. Yes, you heard that correctly. I was being assigned to a place where mental illness was a factor in the inmates' lives.

In my brief days of stay and careful observation by the prison staff, I was called into the warden's office. In this initial exchange, they commented, "Stephen, we don't see any evidence of you having any mental illness problems. What was the situation surrounding the prior warden's declaration to send you here?" With an open mind and a willingness to learn, I shared with the warden the circumstances and context behind my prior conversation with Dianne. I was not a threat to myself, and I was not having suicidal thoughts. He understood my story.

From that day forward, I had a great working relationship with the warden. He advised that I get involved with helping those inmates who genuinely do have mental problems. I was given a job serving their needs. I enjoyed being used by God in this manner. I felt a sense of divine purpose, and it sure made the days more lively and fulfilling. Yes, I was still behind bars and still had many more months of incarceration to my name, but at least the blessings of God were on my stay. Like my time in Williamsburg, SC, I got involved with the church services on Sundays. In North Carolina, I had the opportunity to spearhead the entire service plan. It was so rewarding. I watched inmates come to Christ as Lord and Savior during my years of stay there. During those years, the Spirit of God continued to craft what Soldier for the Cross Ministries would become. I was feeling the hand of God all over my life, and I was grateful for His presence.

Oddly enough, in North Carolina, the months seemed to melt away like butter on a warm roll at dinner time. I knew God was changing me inside out, and my character was becoming more like Jesus Christ. A new "me" was emerging as the Potter formed a vessel for honor. I was fortunate here and wanted to end my prison sentence in this manner. *Nonetheless, God had other plans.*

There arrived another warden at the facility in North Carolina. Let me put it mildly. She and I did not hit it off well. I was respectful and courteous. Yet, it seemed that she did not like me. We had no harmony together. One day, out of nowhere, I was called to her office. She wanted to transfer me out of her facility. I begged and pleaded with her to let me finish my sentence in North Carolina. To no avail, I was told I was being transferred. In a last-ditch attempt to stay, I went over her ranking to request the transfer be denied. That made her all the more disgruntled with me. My ability to stay was closing fast. At this point, I just put it in God's hands. By now, that was easier to do as I was becoming a Disciple of Jesus Christ, not just a fan or casual follower.

Diesel therapy, once again, was heading my way. This transfer would make my third and final stop at the Atlanta Holding Facility. Conditions at this "resort" will never change, as I was learning. I was thankful that this would likely be my last visit to this place. By this time, God had so transformed my heart that I saw inmates as souls and downplayed the conditions of the surroundings. I was going to use this time to share the love of God with those in my cell. It is incredible when God gets a hold of your mind and heart that you look at things differently. It takes on an eternal implication rather than an earthly view. It makes all the difference. These two weeks seemed to fly by as a result.

The final stop of my prison tour would be in Edgefield, South Carolina. While I was not thrilled about the transfer, I sought to make the best of my time there. By this point in my relationship with Christ, I knew that God did not do random things. If I was there, I had to accept that God was up to something that I may not have perceived at the moment. Nevertheless, I was hopeful that I would meet new friends and get plugged into the church life there. God does not make mistakes. I knew He would reveal His plan for this season.

As in my other two locations, Pastor John continued to be an inspiration to me. When I think of his heart for God and his love for me, I get emotional. He was a faithful friend during my incarceration. This verse comes to mind when I think of Pastor John, "A friend loves at all times, and a brother is born for a time of adversity" (Proverbs 17:17 NIV). I also believe every time he visited me for those six years, it seemed random. Still, in truth, it was a perfect appointment orchestrated by the Holy Spirit to comfort me when I was struggling or bringing clarity to a confusing time. God always intimately knew when I needed Pastor John and precisely why in those moments. He would show up to visit and give me a word from the Lord that would carry me and help me grow more in my faith and walk with Him. Our relationship was genuinely saturated in the Holy Spirit of God.

> "But when He, the Spirit of truth, comes, He will guide you into all the truth; for He will not speak on His own initiative, but whatever He hears, He will speak; and He will disclose to you what is to come" (John 16:13 NIV).

These were sincerely divine appointments and touched my heart profoundly and forever. Pastor John always found the time to write to me and visit me when no one else did. He also taught me what it meant to be a man after God's own heart. Pastor John doesn't just talk the talk. He walked the walk daily.

I earnestly love this man and his wife, Connie, as a son would love his mother and father. His precious wife has been fighting for her life for over four years with cancer, and John still finds the time to serve others daily with her blessing. I am saddened to say that Ms. Connie went home to be the Lord in 2020. They were two of the most unselfish people I know.

Connie was a delightful person and a saint to me. I gave her a gift of gratitude for all she had done for me; I made her a custom Bible cover in the prison leather shop. She loved that cover, and to anyone who asked where she got it, she was always proud to tell the story about me. Even my own family did not love me like that. Proverbs 18:24 (NIV) says it all about this godly man and his unselfish wife,

"One who has unreliable friends soon comes to ruin, but there is a friend that sticks closer than a brother."

As in my two previous stints, the Edgefield experience had its ups and downs. Yet, God continued to give me clarity and conviction about my soon exit and what it would look like in the natural. To be honest, I was getting excited about getting out as I now had a vision for a men's ministry called Soldier for the Cross. Since I had time on my hands, no pun intended, I worked on typing my thoughts for Soldier for the Cross. It was a labor of love to put these divine appropriations on paper. It would carry me through to my final days of prison life. As always, God was meeting me in personal and tangible ways.

His final miracle at Edgefield came when I put in a request to join the drug-free program when I was released. If chosen, this would shave off one full year of my sentence and allow me to get back into society. My involvement in the program would be monitored, but I could do it as a civilian and get back to some level of everyday living. I earnestly prayed that God would open this door for me. When I mentioned this opportunity to Pastor John and who would be running the program, he stated he knows the person personally. He said, "If you can get a letter of accommodation and I write a letter of recommendation, then maybe we can get you in the program." We set out to put these letters together and get them submitted. As the time passed, I was prayerful that God would touch the heart of the program director.

I cannot tell you how delighted I was to find out that God moved on this situation, and I got chosen for the program. Did I tell you, "It cut off twelve months of my prison sentence!" It did! When I think of having been given one hundred and eight months of prison time and only having to serve eighty-four of those months, I have to give God praise. While seven years is still a long time, at least it was not nine years. God showed me mercy, and I was duly grateful to Him.

As my days came to a close, I was released on a cold, windy day in early February 2014. No long parade was waiting for my arrival as the guest of honor. No fireworks show to commemorate my release and new freedom. None of that for me. I quietly packed up my "proverbial" tent and went on my way. Was I ready for the challenge of rebuilding my world? I genuinely believed I was. Why? God had met me. And, I had met God! Together, we were going to get a "do-over." I was in for a divine reboot, and this time, Jesus Christ would be my center and foundation. Was I a little unsure of what lay ahead? You bet! Did I know that the Creator of the Universe had my life all mapped out? You bet I did! It is quite alright to trust an "unknown" future to a "known" God. Excited and humbled, I would enter society once again. Let us learn how God met me while starting over as I got back in the REAL world in Chapter 23. Before getting there, I want to share about Soldier for the Cross and the New Me. Read on, my dear friend!

KEEPING IT REAL!

1. The Atlanta Holding Facility. Why did this shock me at first?

2. Diesel Therapy—Why did the system move the inmates around so much? Was that healthy?

3. Mental Health Issue—They thought I was suicidal which sent him to NC. How does God use events to position us?

4. While at the Edgefield prison, God was able to shave off one year of my sentence. How?

5. I led services and joined the choir. How was God reshaping me behind bars?

~ Verse to Memorize ~

[1] Listen as Wisdom calls out! Hear as understanding raises her voice! [2] On the hilltop along the road, she takes her stand at the crossroads. -Proverbs 8:1–2 (NLT)

21

SOLDIER FOR THE CROSS

My time spent in prison was a soul-searching time. I honestly never believed this would be a part of my narrative. As a police officer, I was the one who put "criminals" behind bars. Now, I found myself living in a prison cell for what would feel like an eternity. Amid everything negative, God was stirring in my life, and I could not deny it. When time is on your side, you ponder your whole life's story. In the end, God downloaded into me a destiny that I never dreamed of, and it excited my heart. It gave me hope! It gave me a purpose for the rest of my days.

The Bible is clear about who and what God has called us to be in Christ Jesus: A Soldier for the Cross. It is recorded in 2 Timothy 2:1–4 (NIV),

> "2 You then, my son, be strong in the grace that is in Christ Jesus. 2 And the things you have heard me say in the presence of many witnesses entrust to reliable people who will also be qualified to teach others. 3 Join with me in suffering, like a good soldier of Christ Jesus. 4 No one serving as a soldier gets entangled in civilian affairs, but rather tries to please his commanding officer."

In this passage, the Apostle Paul instructs his young protégé how to live his life for God. First, the senior mentor tells young Timothy to be strong in Christ Jesus. The clear mandate here is to recognize your TRUE source in this life. *Men, when left to your strength, you will always fall into temptation and sin.* Do not fool yourself! Your flesh does not play fair. Yet, in the power of Jesus Christ, you can overcome the schemes of the devil.

Next, the Apostle Paul is admonishing Timothy to pour into himself the knowledge of the living God such that he would then be able to invest his learnings into others. *Men, God is asking you to take your spiritual life and its growth seriously.* Yes, you may exclaim that you are not religious, or your wife is the Bible leader in your home. Can I be honest with you here? That is NOT God's order. God calls you to be the Spiritual Head over your wife, children, and home. *You do not get a pass on this.* What a difference my life would have been had my father been that to my mom and brothers. I cannot overstate this point. It is a matter of life and death to everyone you love. *Lean into it.*

Thirdly, Timothy is told to endure suffering like a Good Soldier of Jesus Christ. In other words, you will have challenges in this life that you were not expecting and were not prepared to handle. Why? The devil is trying to sideline you for good. He has a bullseye on your back, and he does not play fair. *Men, it would be best if you were prepared to handle life's ups and downs.* It is going to come into your world. *Expect it!* What the Apostle Paul is careful to share is that life has its casualties. It hurts. It wounds. It destroys. It can leave you bloody in the wake of its attempts to knock you out. However, keep on training as a good soldier. Always know that you need to engage in your preparation daily. As I write this today, I am reminded of the host of mental bruises I received as a teenager. My dysfunctional family was riddled with suffering and pain. At that age, you are not thinking about being a soldier. Instead, you are thinking about being a survivor. Yet, I cannot help but wonder if I was more pursuant in my relationship with God if I had overcome those mental blows that left me devastated and damaged.

Finally, young Timothy is told to keep his focus on the mission: Living for God. An excellent parallel is given to compare what grabs our attention. If you are a Soldier for the Cross, the Apostle Paul warns, do not get entangled with civilian life affairs. In other words, you cannot live with one foot on the soldier's life and one foot on civilian life. *Men, here is the million-dollar question, "Do you live your life as a double-minded man?"* Do you have one foot on God and the other foot on the world? You come to church on Sunday, but you check out on God the other six days of the week? Be honest. If that is how you live, I want to give you some tools and truths to bolster your walk with God and put Him entirely at the front of your focus. You need both feet squarely on your relationship with Jesus Christ.

Why did I feel compelled to start Soldier for the Cross Ministries? Why was my life being redirected by God to invest all of my energies into this effort? That is simple to answer, as noted by the Apostle Paul's guidance from our text.

1. Your Strength comes from God alone.
2. Your Growth in God is essential daily.
3. Your Sufferings are temporary as a Soldier of Christ.
4. Your Focus must be fixed solely on God.

God showed me these four areas of deficiency about my own life before coming to prison and the life of every other person in the prison system with me. That lack of mentoring is why every prisoner ends up here in these four walls called a cell. Sadly, this is factual no matter the age, color, socio-economic background, cultural affiliation, or education level. A lack of guidance while young will profoundly affect your judgment and decision-making skills in the future. Additionally, it will create a weakness in choosing healthy, godly friendships over the "riff-raff" kinds of people you are likely to associate yourself with.

God moved on my heart to create a ministry where the above four ingredients could be added to every male life, no matter the initial foundation. These four tenets would be the litmus test for how a man was developing and growing into a God-fearing individual and Soldier for the Cross. I am committed to making sure no one, young or old, ends up behind bars because he has not heard the truth of the Gospel of Jesus Christ and the values of what the Apostle Paul was teaching his rising student, Timothy.

If I can live the rest of my days giving hope to men around this globe, God can impart to their storyline a belief that where one starts in life is not where he has to end up. *I am living proof of that, myself.* God is still rewriting our misfortunes for His eternal outcome. Soldier for the Cross Ministries is my gift back to Him. Who would have ever believed that the ideas and processes of fleshing out this ministry were birthed behind the iron structures that took my own freedom? Yes, it was the culmination of thought and prayer through a duration of eighty-four months of living in a precarious place called Prison Town, USA. Yet, God ALWAYS gets the last word over your life, just like He had mine. Never forget that. Soldiers for the Cross arise!

Let's list these beliefs one more time:

1. Your Strength comes from God alone.
2. Your Growth in God is essential daily.
3. Your Sufferings are temporary as a Soldier of Christ.
4. Your Focus must be fixed solely on God.

Let us dive into my life changes in Chapter 22, The New Me. I recorded my thoughts as I was getting ready to go home. Let these words of life encourage your soul. If this can happen to me, it can certainly be your story and hope, too.

KEEPING IT REAL!

1. Soldier for the Cross Ministries was birthed in prison. What can God do in your life that seems unlikely at the time?

2. Paul loved mentoring Timothy. Would you be open to having a mentor? How would it impact your life?

3. Of the four ingredients for spiritual growth, which one do you do the best with? Which one needs work? What will you do to bolster growth?

4. Men, God can change a checkered past. What about your life would you like to see changed? Why?

5. I wanted to live for God each day now. Do you find your purpose in God?

~ Verse to Memorize ~

[25] Let your eyes look straight ahead; fix your gaze directly before you. [26] Give careful thought to the paths for your feet and be steadfast in all your ways. [27] Do not turn to the right or the left; keep your foot from evil. -Proverbs 4:25–27 (NIV)

22

THE NEW ME

Stephen L. Harrison Sr. 78434-004
Edgefield Federal Prison Camp
Unit D-l
PO Box 72
Edgefield, South Carolina, 29284

The New Me

I first want to give all the glory, honor, and praise to my Lord and Savior Jesus Christ because with Him, all things are indeed possible, and because without Him in my life, I can do nothing. I was led to write this by the Holy Spirit because I am a new "me" in Christ Jesus. For those who have been praying for me over these past six years, it worked. I wanted you to know what God has done in my life. These words that I write are my own and from a book I was inspired to read.

As I look back on these six and a half years of my life in prison, I realize I would have never made it if it had not been for God. As I walked through these years of my life and the tragedy of divorce and losing my family, job, and integrity, I found myself in the Israelites' story. I don't mean that I read the story a lot. I mean that I identified very much with the Israelites and their plight through my own life. I now know first-hand about suffering, and I experienced it personally. However, I could see, at the time, how God was providing and protecting me through it.

The story of the Israelites, at the Red Sea, has truly blessed me. They had just been released from captivity and were heading away from Egypt. When they reached the Red Sea, with mountains on either side, they looked back and saw the Egyptian army fast approaching. It must have seemed like a hopeless situation. Given the same circumstance, I am sure I would have been questioning God's plan too.

As I saw my family falling apart, from my incarceration and my wife's choice to divorce, I found myself wondering about God's good and perfect plan and was questioning Him as to why all this was happening to me. I understood those poor, hurting, and terrified Israelites. Their story's beauty is that God was already making a way through their crisis before they even knew they needed it. Truthfully, He was already making one for me too.

The Lord parted the waters of the Red Sea to provide them an escape route. The Bible, in Exodus 14:21 says, "that the Lord drove back the sea with a strong east wind," which implies that the wind came from the other shoreline toward them. Can you see the glorious wonder in that? God parted the water toward them, not away from them. He was making the path for their escape before they even could see it. *God brought it to them.* "Did you hear that?" God is making ways for all of us, even now! When we don't know what it's going to look like or when it's going to come, we can still see God's plan for our lives unfolding. And, His plan is far more significant and better than any outcomes we can ever imagine! There is so much to the Red Sea story. I love what God said to Israel through Moses. While the Israelites were freaking out, which is a normal response for them (and me, too), God told them:

"Fear not, stand firm, and see the salvation of the Lord, which he will work for you today. For the Egyptians whom you see today, you shall never see again. The Lord will fight for you, and you have only to be silent" (Exodus 14:13–14).

That was a word for me that I wish I would have listened to, heard, and applied in my life early on. I'm not sure what "Hush. Be still and watchful," is most of the time. In his book, *My Utmost for His Highest*, Oswald Chambers wrote a devotional that blessed my heart. He said, "If we believe in Jesus, it is not that God makes us beautifully rounded grapes, but that He squeezes the sweetness out of us." Spiritually, we cannot measure our life by success, but only by what God pours through us, and we cannot measure that at all.

In the Scriptures, it states, "He that believeth in me, out of him shall flow rivers of living water." As a result, hundreds of other lives will be continually refreshed. *It is time now to break my life, to cease craving for satisfaction, and spill the thing out.* I love the visual of round, plump grapes being squeezed so that the lovely, sweet juice flows out. I pray that my life would be marked by the sweetness of Christ spilling from my thoughts, actions, and words. I'm afraid that sometimes the only thing spilling from me is myself. I know that God has good intentions for me. I wish that He defined "good" the same way that I do.

Here's my definition: Good means no pain, no sorrow, no betrayal, no sacrifices: everyone does what I ask when I ask it; I have time for everything I want to do; people love me; I get to do whatever I want; nobody is "stupid"; my sons grow up and are perfect: I'm happily married; I'm madly in love with my new wife, and more importantly, she's in love with me. Although I think God would say most of those things are right, I don't believe that those things are measures of the good He wants to do in my life.

His definition would most likely look like this: Good is whatever draws you closer to Me and makes you more like Me. It allows you to experience the beauty of trusting Me and showing you that I love you too much to make you *happy* because I long to make you *holy*. It's difficult, after a personal tragedy, for anyone to get to a place where you think, "God, I trust You completely. I know that You will get me through anything, even if it's another nightmare!" That's not so easy to say either. I know it wasn't for me. I spent many a month waiting for the next disaster to strike.

I know that sounds a bit crazy, but because something horrible happened to me, like going to prison for nine years, it was easier to think that God was going to keep beating me until I got whatever He wanted me to get. I finally realized that this wasn't God's way at all. *God used this difficulty to refine me, strengthen me, and ultimately bless me, not punish me.*

Many people would remind me of James 1:2–4 that "I should count it all joy" to suffer, that suffering is sharing in an experience with Christ, and it is truly a gift. I always wanted to respond, "Are you serious? Really?" (Word of Advice: Don't say this to someone in prison or who's going through a divorce!) I laugh about it now as I look back at all those days, weeks, months, and years of pain, of the feeling of betrayal and being forgotten.

Today, I see a more peaceful man in the making. I know a man who is so much closer to the Lord than I ever thought possible, a man who loves the Lord, who's hungry for the things of God. I am a man who has learned to walk with a measure of grace that has only come from the Holy Spirit. But, when things went from bad to worse, I became fearful because they did most of the time. I was afraid of failing at this new path that God had called me to walk on. And yet, I knew that God wouldn't give me more than His grace would allow me to bear. His purpose for my life was never to destroy me, but to provide me with just enough, not "too much," so that I turned to him. I know now that I can only do this life, depending entirely on Him.

Jesus isn't a "break-glass-when-needed" kind of Savior, even though that's what I did most of the time in my life when I was in trouble or in need of something. Jesus is to me a "need-You-every-millisecond" Savior and a "don't-try-this-alone Savior." For me, by relying on Him, I can do this life. It might be messy at times, but my life will be well-lived messes that will glorify God.

Amid abandonment, divorce, and imprisonment, I think it was vital to share how difficult this path was for me. It was demanding and challenging, and it's easy to be overwhelmed. At times, I got discouraged and looked away from God as if there was a better option than God. I've come to realize, in my life, that there is no other option for me than God. He is it for me. *I can't even imagine living this life without the Lord's peace and hope.*

God used this experience, in my life, to make me more like Christ. Each day, He poured His spirit into my life with abandonment and lavished me with His love. It truly is the best love out there, no matter what the world tells you about romance. Today's "world" offers the view of love that comes in all shapes and sizes, but romantic love is a counterfeit. I have come to understand more and more each day that His love is REAL love.

Jesus is more than willing and able to take your burdens, more than willing to carry you, more than hopeful that you will allow Him to be your Savior. Allowing Him into my life each day wasn't easy. Trying to handle everything independently and trying to figure things out were very overwhelming moments for me. I thank God for every one of those moments because it made me the man I am today. I have come to realize that my lifelong blessings lie in a heart that hopes in the Lord's steadfast love and trusts that God only allows in our lives those things that will make us better, healthier, and more able to bless others. I want to be that kind of man. I want my sons to rise and call me blessed and my friends and neighbors to be inspired by my life, inspired to know Christ. I want people to see Jesus instead of me. I want people to not even think about me as much as they feel about Him because they know He is my identity.

This new me will occasionally be a stumbling, fumbling mess of a sinner, but I'm on the road to knowing my Savior better each day. I'm determined that I will run this race that is set before me with grace, faith, and strength from the Lord, but most of all, His love. I might feel weak, inadequate, fearful, and anxious, but I know "God is the strength of my heart and my portion forever." I believe I can do all that He has called me to do.

So who am I going to become in this life? What kind of man, husband, father, friend? How am I going to survive? I'll tell you how! I'm going to speak God's word into my life and get it firmly into my head, but mostly in my heart. I'm going to be a man who walks with his head held high because I know that God's love is unfailing. I'm going to be a man who isn't afraid of the future because I trust that God has it all handled, and it's going to be good. I'm not going to be a man worried about my sons because I know God loves them just as He loves me. I'm going to be a man who doesn't fear loneliness because I have my constant companion and friend, Jesus.

I want to be:

- A man of faith
- A man of the Word
- A quiet and gentle-spirited man
- A man who holds his tongue
- A man who listens
- A man who overflows with the fruit of the Spirit: love, joy, peace, patience, kindness, goodness, faithfulness, gentleness, and self-control
- A man whose children know they are loved and feel nurtured
- A man whose children are devoted to God
- A man whose home is organized, inviting, and loving
- A man whose finances are in order

- A man whose life is a reflection of God's faithfulness
- A man who is useful to his friends
- A handsome man
- A worshipful man
- A loving man
- A man who bears with others
- A man who is physically fit
- A man who is healthy, emotionally, physically, and spiritually
- A man who knows his Savior loves him
- A man who is secure in his walk with the Lord
- A man whose children know the Lord and study His Word
- A man who seeks the Lord
- A man who shares his gifts, wisdom, and possessions
- A man who is forgiving and loved

Each day, I'm genuinely blessed to sense God leading me still. I will rely on the Lord to show me how to best restore and raise my sons with strength and joy. Because I have a personal relationship with the Lord, I'll never truly feel alone. *Sometimes, I still struggle, even after I pray, study, and seek wise counsel. Sometimes, the answers don't come instantly; but that's when I must exercise my faith and trust what I don't see, believing what I don't always feel, and hoping for better things to come.*

I might still have moments and feelings of being overwhelmed, but I only need to bow my head and seek God's peace to find comfort in my times of trouble. In this world, the Lord has said that we will have many trials and tribulations in our life, but He said to be of good joy because He overcame them all. I do not know what the future holds for me and how to handle a particular situation or make a confident decision. But, I know that I will find the correct answer when I seek His help through prayer, His Word, and godly counsel for all my concerns. I know I will feel sorrow and deep pain over all that has happened, but

God has comforted me through His Word and the kindness and love of friends and family.

I know that recovering from the hurt of divorce, adultery, and abandonment is still an uphill battle for me, but the struggle no longer belongs to me. It belongs to God. He is trustworthy, and He will never leave me or forsake me. God has a perfect plan for my life, and I know it will be fulfilled. I know He will do great things in my life as I continue to place my trust in Him. God bless you and thank you for all your prayers, love, and support over these past years. *The best is yet to come.*

Love Always,

Steve

Wow! When I look back over those declarations, it brings tears to my eyes, even many years later. The Lord was plowing some ground in my heart for good soil to emerge. Also, He was renewing my mind in the Word of God and showcasing His promises over my life. **I was a "new" man in Christ Jesus.** While I am constantly "under construction," I strive to live out those tenets today and always. The Lord is my Good Shepherd, and He leads me daily. It reminds me of Psalm 23 we so often quote. While this is primarily a psalm spoken at funerals, it has more to say about everyday life than death. Please read this series of divine promises over your life from God.

Psalm 23
(NLT)

1 The LORD is my shepherd; I have all that I need.
2 He lets me rest in green meadows; he leads me beside peaceful streams.
3 He renews my strength. He guides me along right paths, bringing honor to his name.
4 Even when I walk through the darkest valley, I will not be afraid, for you are close beside me. Your rod and your staff protect and comfort me.
5 You prepare a feast for me in the presence of my enemies. You honor me by anointing my head with oil. My cup overflows with blessings.
6 Surely your goodness and unfailing love will pursue me all the days of my life, and I will live in the house of the LORD forever.

Do those words leap off the page at you? They should. Those are words of life and death. You are never alone, and God is working in your life for soul rest! What a promise. What a Savior and Lord! Let's explore my life as I reenter society as a free man, again in Chapter 23, Back in the REAL world.

KEEPING IT REAL!

1. New things. We all like shiny new things. Why are we so attracted to new things?

2. I was not leaving prison the same way I arrived. How had God transformed me?

3. God's promises bring hope. Which ones stand out to you as you read my declaration?

4. I also thanked my family and friends for their support and prayers while in prison. Why was this so important to include?

5. I said there might be days I "stumble" in my walk with God. What advice would you give me about this?

~ *Verse to Memorize* ~

[21] For the LORD sees clearly what a man does, examining every path he takes. [22] An evil man is held captive by his sins; they are ropes that catch and hold him.
-Proverbs 5:21–22 (NLT)

23

BACK IN THE REAL WORLD

Every incarcerated man dreams of the day of his release, that is, if he gets one. I was no different here. The fact that my prison term was one hundred and eight months shouted there was an expiration date on my lack of freedom. Sure, that is better than life in confinement. Nevertheless, it seemed as though the days moved at a snail's pace. If you put three thousand two hundred and eighty-five marbles in a jar and remove one each day, there would be a conclusion point called RELEASE. For me, that day was July 21, 2014. I had waited so long to get out.

Let me share the "weird" part of my trajectory with you as I headed back into the REAL world. While I was getting my freedom, I left behind a family I had grown to love and cared genuinely for their well-being. Now before you do a double-take and ask, "Stephen, these men, in your wake, are felons! Offenders who have done some terrible things that landed them there in the first place. Why would you be sad to leave them?"

Now, let me be honest. If I had never been put into custody, I would continue to think just like you. Now hold on, I am not judgmental of you, but rather relating to my conclusions about my thinking and the lack of compassion for such individuals. Until you walk and interact daily with these precious souls for whom Christ died, you would think they are also worthy of being discarded. Yes, I said the word discarded, like a paper cup in the trash can. I know as a police officer, my mind would lean toward such beliefs. *However, when I became a convict, I was now ranked among them.* Yet, I was not a wrongful person.

Nevertheless, I just did some questionable stuff. I made an error in my decision-making process. So did my peers, whom my heart profoundly cherished. I could not shake this feeling of intense empathy for my fellow cellmates. I know that sounds mushy, but friends let me cut to the chase. "If it were not for the grace of God, where would you be today? It would be the same place I would be headed, too: Hell." Do not overlook this essential factor in your life's story. This truth is echoed by the Apostle Paul as recorded in Ephesians 2:8–10 (NKJV),

"[8] For by grace you have been saved through faith, and that not of yourselves; *it is* the gift of God, [9] not of works, lest anyone should boast. [10] For we are His workmanship, created in Christ Jesus for good works, which God prepared beforehand that we should walk in them."

Grace. Think of that word for a minute. It is not just what we say at meals, although we do call it that. That is a little meaning for the power and impact of the word, Grace. You can't shake this dynamic fact. *It is ALL about HIS GRACE over your life.* The above passage starts with "For by grace." Just stop right there. Hit your holy pause button. Ponder those three words. Let them sink into your soul and spirit. Why consider Grace? That answer is an easy one for me. It changes EVERYTHING. The next time you are in a quandary about anything negative, stop, say to yourself, "For by grace," and fill in the blank. It will shift the atmosphere and your future thinking.

Next, think of the conclusion of such a statement as found in verses 8 and 9. Through faith, and with no help of my own, I can be saved from Hell's punishment and Satan's grip. And, yes, Heaven can be my eternal home. It is that simple, but it is not simplistic. It is a profound mystery why the Living God would love me and you that much. But, He does! I do not have to work for His approval. I cannot even earn it, even if I wanted to or was willing to give it my best shot. No, it is a GIFT. Salvation is a gift from God to you. Your part is straightforward, "Are you willing to receive that gift of LOVE?" I did, and I have never been the same since. Sadly, many do not, and that breaks God's heart.

Lastly, verse 10 is what I would call my response to God's goodness of salvation. As His artistry, I am to offer my life to His mandate of good works to benefit others. God desires me and you to walk out what He has put in. That seems like a reasonable request from our Loving, Heavenly Father. In profound gratitude and thankfulness to God, I awake every day with a drive and conviction to lift His name and express my love for Him as His workmanship. A transformed life can't help but serve Jesus Christ as your Savior and Lord.

Okay, back to my prison contemporaries and the need for a redemptive story over their lives. Discardable? Hardly! Why? Because God's "For by grace," power has not changed. When you whisper for God's grace to come running your way, its power can rescue and change the worst of circumstances. Yes, even inmates can experience the undeniable power of God's grace to renovate their lives. Is that not what it's all about anyway? I was leaving prison an altered man. I knew it. The guards knew it—my family knew it. And guess what, the whole world was about to realize it, too. If you have ever been touched with "For by grace," you will be a walking billboard for God's gentle touch over your life.

My peers were not misfits in a holding place for eternity to erase. No, no, no! The redemptive hand of God longed to go into each cell and give them new hearts. Hearts made of flesh, tender toward God and yielding to His divine directives. Everyone deserves to know that God can create beauty from ashes, despite what things may look like at the moment. As I prepared for my release, I can remember that I wanted to come back somehow to rescue my friends from death's grip and Hell's hideout. As a Soldier for the Cross, I committed to God that much like the Terminator, Arnold Schwarzenegger, made famous the "I will be back!" line that somehow, I would return to share the love of Jesus Christ to prisoners the world over.

I just wanted to share the above declaration. No prisoner can leave a prison system and not take part of that system with him as well as the faces of those who helped chronicle his days and nights. It is much like the children of Israel, leaving Egypt for the first time. Egypt, at some level, was in their DNA. It would take decades for God to purge this ideology out of their beings. I can truthfully say the same about my life as I made my way back into society.

For starters, I was in need financially. As you could imagine, being behind bars for seven years, I needed to get back on my feet resourcefully. I knew I could rebuild my financial nest egg, but it would take some time to do so. I was thrifty and always had an entrepreneurial bent so my mind was always spinning with ideas to make money. Thank goodness, I could once again use my talents to generate revenue. I was rearing to go.

Next, I had to make peace with where my family had deteriorated too. Truthfully, the hardest thing for me was the loss of my marriage and valuable time with my two boys. You can't get back that time and children need it so badly. Nevertheless, I was determined to begin investing again in my sons, as they gave me an opportunity. Yes, it would take time for healing and certainly, trust had to be rebuilt as their father, but I was going to do all I could to create a healthy, and responsive future.

Lastly, as you already heard, I went into prison as a happily married man, but the toll of prison life wearied Dianne and allowed her heart to shrink in love for me. While not my desired end, I know the time away from her was hard on both of us. It was a hard pill that I would have to swallow as I exited my penitentiary sentence, back into the norms of everyday society.

Nonetheless, what God did for me in the jailhouse would not allow worldly circumstances to get me down or distract me from my calling and purpose moving forward. In a day with His favor over my life, God can do what my hands would take decades to acquire. No, I was resolute to keep seeking Him first as recorded in Matthew 6:33 (NCV),

> "*33 Seek first God's kingdom and what God wants. Then all your other needs will be met as well.*"

With this verse as my marching orders as a Soldier for the Cross, I would pursue each day with prayer and thankfulness. God began to open doors for financial opportunities, and I was making a comeback into civilian life. My buddy, Jack Owoc, owner of Bang Energy Drink, allowed me to work in his sales department as my first paying job after my incarceration. Boy, was I ever grateful to Jack and his trust in me as an employee, not to mention his faith in me as his friend! As I said, we go way back as peers and workout mates. To this day, Jack and I are close, and we communicate often. It was my start on the road to purpose and God's best over my life.

I have to be honest. These early days were a bit clunky and awkward at first. It is like relearning to ride a bike again. You know how to do it, but you have been out of practice for some time. Yet, little by little, the expertise comes back. That is what it was like for me as I re-entered the workforce. I was determined to make it, and I pressed on daily with God's provision over my life. I look back now, over six years later, and scratch my head. God has been so gracious and so good to me. I cannot deny His presence in my day-to-day activities.

Today, I am the owner of my own company, and I serve my community with excellence and honesty. Each opportunity to get in front of people is my chance to share my story of redemption and God's mercy over my life. I like to think that I use my daily job to get an audience to share the Gospel of Jesus Christ. That is what I call a "win-win." The Lord has blessed me in every way since leaving prison. I now live in Atlanta, Georgia. I have a beautiful home that is completely paid off. I am part of a thriving men's ministry and prayer ministry. Every chance I get, I am pursuing God with all my heart. Not out of duty, but rather love and obedience. Yes, my life is rich with peace, joy, contentment, and hope. How is that for being back in the <u>REAL</u> world? *I am still pinching myself.* My God is so GOOD to me!

KEEPING IT REAL!

1. "These men are felons." Why was it hard for me to leave?
2. I loved these men. How had God changed my heart about them?
3. I faced some real-life challenges when I got out. How did I now cope?
4. Jack Owoc gave me my first job. How did Jack help here? I was deeply touched. How?
5. Starting over takes faith. How had my faith in God matured?

~ Verse to Memorize ~

⁶ Leave your simple ways behind, and begin to live; learn to use good judgment." ⁷ Anyone who rebukes a mocker will get an insult in return. Anyone who corrects the wicked will get hurt.
-Proverbs 9:5–6 (NLT)

24

POINTING MEN TO JESUS

This mandate in my life to share Jesus Christ with every man I meet, both in prison and in the public sector, has one primary filter: **Keep It Real.** Let me repeat that mantra in another way. To make men consider the life-changing claims of Christ and his powerful truths, I let them know that in everything, we, as Soldiers for the Cross, will operate with honesty, transparency, vulnerability, and authenticity. There is no pretense, superficial masks, Christian happy faces, or religious cloaks of piety among our ranks.

We will embrace our humanness and our failings as part of who we are as men bought with the precious blood of Jesus Christ. Yes, we are born again, but we still will struggle in this life with sin and temptation. We will fall short daily. Nevertheless, we will never stop loving Jesus and living for the Lord. We will keep training to be good Soldiers of the Lord, Jesus Christ. We are in a war, and our eyes must stay on the prize: Lifting the Name of Jesus Christ. Yet, we do fail, at times, and we are willing to be truthful about that.

My fellow soldiers, you are battling within every moment of your life. Do not kid yourself. Sin is sinister, and it is after your life. Look how it is penned in Genesis 4:6–7 (NIV), "⁶ Then the LORD said to Cain, 'Why are you angry? Why is your face downcast? ⁷ If you do what is right, will you not be accepted? But if you do not do what is right, sin is crouching at your door; it desires to have you, but you must rule over it.'" Wow! That verse gives me holy chills every time I read it. Sin is seen here as a monster, waiting to trample its prey. It desires to have you! Do not overlook that. That should create a holy fear in your soul.

Sin wants to bring you and me down, to have us sidelined and ineffective as Soldiers for the Cross. We must resist evil, firm in our faith in Jesus Christ as shared in James 4:4–10 (MSG),

> "[4-6] You're cheating on God. If all you want is your own way, flirting with the world every chance you get, you end up enemies of God and his way. And do you suppose God doesn't care? The proverb has it that 'he's a fiercely jealous lover.' And what he gives in love is far better than anything else you'll find. It's common knowledge that 'God goes against the willful proud; God gives grace to the willing humble.'
>
> "[7-10] So let God work his will in you. Yell a loud *no* to the Devil and watch him scamper. Say a quiet *yes* to God and he'll be there in no time. Quit dabbling in sin. Purify your inner life. Quit playing the field. Hit bottom, and cry your eyes out. The fun and games are over. **Get serious, really serious.** *Get down on your knees before the Master; it's the only way you'll get on your feet."* (Bold and Italics added)

Those last two sentences are paramount for living a life pleasing to God. "Get down on your knees" is an act of surrender and yielding to the Lord's will over your life. It says "no" to the flesh and its longings and "yes" to the Holy Spirit who lives inside of you, drawing you to the Father's will. This Scripture then goes on to say, "it is the only way you will get on your feet." That is an absolute truth. Humility is a launching pad, not a place of personal weakness. Many will shout at you and say you are foolish for such relinquish of your will, but God gives His grace to the humble. You may wonder how all of this is possible. It would help if you grabbed hold of the bold admonition listed above: **Get serious, really serious.** Ponder that for a minute. Would you be able to say, "I am serious, really serious about my relationship with God? Do you even have one?" Most men dismiss the spiritual component of their lives and charter, a course they take all on their own. When the chips fall and usually do, he comes running to God for help and hope. Let us turn the corner on this superficial way of living. Give God space in your life for a change. Why? Sin kills! And, it hurts everyone you love.

The Apostle Paul, responsible for writing almost two-thirds of the entire New Testament, had this to say about his battle against sin and his walk with the Lord, Jesus Christ. He calls it: The War Within. This battle is found in Romans 7: 14–25 (NCV),

> "[14] We know that the law is spiritual, but I am not spiritual since sin rules me as if I were its slave. [15] I do not understand the things I do. I do not do what I want to do, and I do the things I hate. [16] And if I do not want to do the hated things I do, that means I agree that the law is good. [17] But I am not really the one who is doing these hated things; it is sin living in me that does them. [18] Yes, I know that nothing good lives in me—I mean nothing good lives in the part of me that is earthly and sinful. I want to do the things that are good, but I do not do them. [19] I do not do the good things I want to do, but I do the bad things I do not want to do. [20] So if I do things I do not want to do, then I am not the one doing them. It is sin living in me that does those things.
>
> "[21] So I have learned this rule: When I want to do good, evil is there with me. [22] In my mind, I am happy with God's law. [23] But I see another law working in my body, which makes war against the law that my mind accepts. That other law working in my body is the law of sin, and it makes me its prisoner.

²⁴ What a miserable man I am! Who will save me from this body that brings me death? ²⁵ I thank God for saving me through Jesus Christ our Lord!"

So, how do we point men to Jesus Christ? We share the above verses and offer complete honesty about our walk with the Lord. Let us face facts. We will all have bad days. We will blow it while trying to live for God. We will sin and cause hurt to others that we love. We will embrace the sinful nature that battles the spiritual heart and wonder if we will ever be free from the effects of sinfulness. If you have ever wondered about that, then you are in good company. The Apostle Paul said this of himself as listed above, *"²⁴ What a miserable man I am! Who will save me from this body that brings me death? ²⁵ I thank God for saving me through Jesus Christ our Lord."* There you have the Apostle Paul's remedy for the war within. It is ONLY Jesus Christ who will be able to help you conquer an evil nature. Until you go home to be with the Lord, this internal battle rages continually.

Flesh vs. Spirit is constant warfare in your life. With a posture of reverence and awe for God and a mind that gets renewed daily, you can press on. This encouragement is noted in Philippians 4:12–14 (NIV), *"¹² Not that I have already obtained all this, or have already arrived at my goal, but I press on to take hold of that for which Christ Jesus took hold of me. ¹³ Brothers and sisters, I do not consider myself yet to have taken hold of it. But one thing I do: Forgetting what is behind and straining toward what is ahead, ¹⁴ I press on toward the goal to win the prize for which God has called me heavenward in Christ Jesus."* Did you catch that advice from the Scriptures? 1.) Forget the Past. 2.) Embrace the Present. 3.) Press on toward the Future. This prescription seems relevant, tangible, and doable. Would you consider such a proclamation for growing in your faith in God? It works, my brothers in the Lord. It truly works!

Pointing men to Jesus involves the greatest of ingredients: *Love.* Why Love, you may wonder? Because Love never fails. When Life beats men up along its highway, men come to a place where they either need love or an escape. The escape is usually a destructive approach to medicate life's pain, setbacks, hurts, challenges, and shortcomings. It will include alcohol, drugs, pornography, workaholism, sexual activity, gambling, and other addictive vices. They trap you and numb you momentarily. However, they offer no lasting kind of relief. It is an illusion that Satan offers to all willing patrons.

Contrast that with LOVE, God's love. This kind of love is a healing, contagious type of love. It is shown through relationships with other godly men doing life together. In these small group settings, we talk about pain, setbacks, hurts, challenges, and inadequacies. No, we do not dismiss them, but we do look at them from a higher vantage point: the Word of God. What does the Holy Bible say about one's present situations, and how can you grow through this difficulty? What would you do differently moving forward? Is the Holy Spirit trying to speak to your heart about a behavior that needs to change? Brothers bounce God's Word with other brothers in an atmosphere of LOVE, sharing what the Scriptures teach about a particular dilemma, problem, or circumstance. This dialogue offers encouragement, equipping, and empowerment for Christ-centered living. Throw in the ingredients of our *Keep It Real* mantra: honesty, transparency, vulnerability, and authenticity, and the outcome is men becoming like Jesus.

Little by little, day by day, and year by year, men become fully committed Soldiers for the Cross of Jesus Christ. Then, we go out to the highways and byways of life and compel men, everywhere, to give their heart to the Lord. It is what the Bible calls *The Ministry of Reconciliation* as chronicled in 2 Corinthians 5:11–15 (NIV),

> "[11] Since, then, we know what it is to fear the Lord, we try to persuade others. What we are is plain to God, and I hope it is

also plain to your conscience. *¹² We are not trying to commend ourselves to you again, but are giving you an opportunity to take pride in us, so that you can answer those who take pride in what is seen rather than in what is in the heart. ¹³ If we are 'out of our mind,' as some say, it is for God; if we are in our right mind, it is for you. ¹⁴ For Christ's love compels us, because we are convinced that one died for all, and therefore all died. ¹⁵ And he died for all, that those who live should no longer live for themselves but for him who died for them and was raised again.*"

My dear brothers in the Lord, let me end with this thought about pointing men to Jesus. Like the Apostle Paul, I am compelled to share the hope of Jesus Christ with everyone I meet. Yes, some think "I am out of my mind" as they did the Apostle Paul. That is fine with me. Yet, I know this one thing. While serving time in federal prison, my life was radically transformed from death to life. Through His Son, Jesus Christ, the Love of God so touched my heart and soul that I am persuaded that everyone needs Jesus in their lives as Savior and Lord. Thus, my life will end its days by pointing men to Jesus and making Soldiers for the Cross. *What an honor!*

KEEPING IT REAL!

1. Keep It Real—Why do men like this approach to life and faith?
2. Embrace your humanness! Do you struggle to accept the *REAL* you? Why?
3. Flesh vs. Spirit. This tug of war is a constant. How do you navigate this battle?
4. God's love motivates. Do you sense His love in your life? How?
5. "Thus, my life will end its days by pointing men to Jesus and making Soldiers for the Cross." How will you end your days?

~ Verse to Memorize ~

⁶The righteousness of the upright will rescue them, But the treacherous will be caught by *their own* greed.
-Proverbs 11: 5–6 (NASB)

25

WAS IT WORTH IT ALL?

I get asked the question all the time, "Was it worth it all?" To be honest, I have pondered this myself from every angle. My meeting Jesus Christ in an amazingly personal way? Absolutely! My losing my marriage and time with my two sons for a total of seven years? That one still stings me deeply, even today. I loved my wife and adored my two boys. They were my life and world. No, I did not idolize them, but they were my inspiration each day for working so hard to provide for them. We were making wonderful family memories together. It is what made life so enjoyable. So, the *truthful* answer is one of "bitterness and sweetness" combined.

Let's begin with the "sweet" part of the question as my love for God is so real, encapsulating, and permanent. No half-hearted Christianity for me. Stephen Lynch Harrison is a changed man. No, not prison reform, but the Holy Spirit transformed kind. There is a HUGE difference, you know! At my core, my life has been made brand new. It could not be expressed in any other way than that a spiritual rebirth as echoed in 2 Corinthians 5:17–20 (MSG),

> "Now we look inside, and what we see is that anyone united with the Messiah (Jesus Christ) gets a fresh start, is created new. The old life is gone; a new life burgeons! Look at it! All

this comes from the God who settled the relationship between us and him, and then called us to settle our relationships with each other. God put the world square with himself through the Messiah, giving the world a fresh start by offering forgiveness of sins. God has given us the task of telling everyone what he is doing. We're Christ's representatives. God uses us to persuade men and women to drop their differences and enter into God's work of making things right between them. We're speaking for Christ himself now: Become friends with God; he's already a friend with you."

My life now had a divine purpose, as spelled out in the above Scriptures. It is no longer just about me acquiring a family, living in a lovely home, driving a nice car, vacationing in the Gulf of Mexico, and retiring with a police pension. Now, I am an Ambassador for the cause of Christ Jesus. I am in the LORD's Army. Or, as I like to put it in Stephen's terms, "I am a Soldier for the Cross." Yes, that is my mission now. I am a Soldier. Nothing more. Nothing Less. I am a soldier for the most significant cause on Planet Earth, the salvation of the souls of men. We are in a war, and I am training daily to be the best I can for Jesus Christ.

Guess what? I am also in the recruiting business as I have been called to gather my brothers worldwide to join this mission by surrendering their own lives to Christ. He is the only name that brings salvation to humanity, as noted in Acts 4:12 (KJV),

"[12] Neither is there salvation in any other: for there is none other name under heaven given among men, whereby we must be saved."

So, my life as a soldier involves fighting and recruiting! I am fighting for the salvation of all men and compelling them to surrender their lives to the King of Kings and Lord of Lords, Jesus Christ. What could cause more passion and purpose than that? Each day when my feet hit the floor, I know God ordains this day and that I have lives that need to know of His saving grace. Yes, I may be selling gutters when I visit customers with each quote, but my undercover work as a soldier is to bring them home to Jesus. Yes, I help men find their way back home to God Almighty. No regrets. No turning back or slowing down. I am on point and purpose for Jesus, my Lord. Have I made that clear? And it gets sweeter every day.

Now for the "bitterness" part of the question. My family life was rich and meaningful for me. I cherished Dianne and the boys as we were amazing together and going somewhere. We were making plans for our future and our forever life together. Make no bones about it; I was a committed husband and an engaged father, unlike the one I had patterned for me. With that said, I watched it slip away as the years in prison rolled on. My sons needed a father, and I was absent from their formidable years for eighty-four months. I can not make that time up, nor will I ever get that back.

In truth, that part hurts me, even to this day. Yes, I have a relationship with my two sons today, but the impact is duly felt, and I am rebuilding. My older son is a little more open and receptive to me than his younger brother. Our relationship is in part because I was sent to prison when he was just seven years old. The elder son was eleven at the time. Notedly, I had more time with my firstborn than the latter. Thankfully, God is helping us rebuild our relational bridges, and each year it is taking shape as it should. For that, I am forever grateful.

As for my darling wife, Dianne? I crushed her spirit and bruised her soul. I truly did! In the beginning, she held on, and I was thankful for her patronage. Nevertheless, as the years rolled along, I believe she got tired, weary, and ultimately lonely for love. While it was not the outcome I hoped for, I do understand her position and emotional framework.

While in prison, Dianne served me with divorce papers to end our marriage. Reluctantly, I signed the documents as it was a means of setting her free to live again. She needed what I could no longer give her behind bars. As I stated, I was sentenced to 108 months in jail but only had to serve time for eighty-four months. Nonetheless, that is 2,555 estranged days and lonely nights. Dianne wanted to wait, but her spirit just could not any longer. I do not fault her. I made choices that negatively impacted her life. She gave me two wonderful sons, and for that, I am indebted to her.

Do you know what I have learned through all of this? Life delivers both bitter and sweet moments every day. Some you get to choose, and some that are just thrust on you. Your only opportunity: the response. Yes, you get to respond to it as God gives you wisdom. They say only 10 percent of what happens to you in life is in your control. The other 90 percent is not in our ability to control. That may frustrate you to some level. Here is the good news. You are 100 percent in control of your responses to life's stressors and challenges. Yes, you get to pick your behavior each time. That is good news.

So, what is my response to *From Cop to Convict to Christ*? Well, I am a work in progress and under construction. God is creating a beautiful masterpiece over my life. Hand-crafted artistry is what God does best. I like the results thus far. Sure, I cannot change things about my story, but I am not sure I would be the same person to rewind the clock. So, what do I do as I move forward? I enjoy the journey as God is still writing my script. My flourishing finish awaits!

> *"There has never been the slightest doubt in my mind that the God who started this great work in you would keep at it and bring it to a flourishing finish on the very day Christ Jesus appears"* (Philippians 1:6 MSG).

KEEPING IT REAL!

1. Was it worth it? That question is always relevant. Is change worth the effort?

2. Sweetness—Life offers sweet things. I tasted the wonders of God. Have you?

3. Bitterness—Life offers bitter things. I lost many things in life. Have you?

4. Life is both bitter and sweet. How do you manage these two extremes?

5. You can control your responses 100 percent of the time. Do you agree? What does God want next from you?

~ Verse to Memorize ~

²A good person basks in the delight of God, and he wants nothing to do with devious schemers. ³You can't find firm footing in a swamp, but life rooted in God stands firm.
-Proverbs 12:2–3 (MSG)

26

MEETING JESUS CHRIST

How to Know Jesus Christ, Personally

All men struggle with being "enough." Admit it! You do. That is where the Shadow of Shame lives. It stalks you daily. It whispers your fears, faults, and failures. Yet, you do not have to live this way. God can redeem your life if you choose Him. If this is your heart's desire, simply pray:

Dear God,

I realize today that I am incomplete and broken by sin. The effects of sin have caused my life to be alienated and far from you. I have drifted along without purpose and joy for way too long. Today, I surrender my heart fully and sincerely to your Son, Jesus Christ. I invite Him into my heart and life to give me a Supreme Makeover: physically, mentally, emotionally, spiritually, and relationally. I endeavor to make Him the number one priority in my life from this day forward. Thank you for giving me a <u>new</u> life and an <u>abundant</u> life. In Jesus Christ's name, I pray and believe. Amen.

Congratulations! You are a new creation!

Now we look inside, and what we see is that anyone united with the Messiah gets a *fresh start, is created new*. The old life is gone; a new life begins! Look at it! All this comes from the God who settled the relationship between us and him, and then called us to settle our relationships with each other (*2 Corinthians 5:17–18 - The Message*).

If you have prayed to receive Jesus Christ personally as Savior and Lord, please email me at **soldier4thecross77@gmail.com** to pray for you!

For Eternity's Sake,

Stephen

Stephen Lynch Harrison Sr.

ABOUT THE AUTHOR

Stephen Lynch Harrison, Sr., established Soldier for the Cross Ministries, Inc. in Atlanta, Georgia. Beyond being a speaker, accomplished business owner, and the host of "The Real Life Real Truth" podcast on his YouTube channel, his genuine zeal lies in disseminating his life-altering narrative, "From Cop to Convict to Christ," to men worldwide. Stephen ardently encourages men to "Keep It Real" about their life circumstances and their profound need for God. For those interested in connecting with Stephen, you can explore his website: www.stephenlynchharrisonsr.com or contact him directly at 470-228-2099.

Thank you for reading my story!

May God Bless You.

Printed in the USA
CPSIA information can be obtained
at www.ICGtesting.com
LVHW091449060524
779122LV00004B/381